Peach Blossom Cologne Company
Short Audit Case

Fourth Edition

Jack W. Paul
Lehigh University

 McGraw-Hill
Irwin

Boston   Burr Ridge, IL   Dubuque, IA   Madison, WI   New York   San Francisco   St. Louis
Bangkok   Bogotá   Caracas   Kuala Lumpur   Lisbon   London   Madrid   Mexico City
Milan   Montreal   New Delhi   Santiago   Seoul   Singapore   Sydney   Taipei   Toronto

McGraw-Hill
Irwin

PEACH BLOSSOM COLOGNE COMPANY: SHORT AUDIT CASE
Jack W. Paul

Published by McGraw-Hill/Irwin, an imprint of The McGraw-Hill Companies, Inc., 1221 Avenue of the Americas, New York, NY 10020. Copyright © 2007 by The McGraw-Hill Companies, Inc. All rights reserved.

Printed in the United States of America.

10 11 12 13 14   QVS/QVS 18 17 16 15 14

ISBN 978-0-07-340396-0
MHID 0-07-340396-2

www.mhhe.com

The McGraw-Hill Companies

Preface

The fourth edition now incorporates materials related to the conduct of an audit of internal control over financial reporting as required by Sarbanes–Oxley. These materials cover internal control analysis, testing, and evaluation, as well as reporting requirements. As in the past, the audit is segmented into business processes. For flexibility in assigning materials, exercises related to the audit of internal control are optional. These exercises can be assigned as time permits. The case is flexible enough to accommodate just a financial statement audit.

If the optional internal control audit exercises are not assigned, the narratives and internal control questionnaires can still be used to prepare flowcharts and assess control risk. After having performed the assessment of control risk, the student will be in a position to write his or her audit program. Prior period working papers are included to provide students with a framework for (1) *designing the current year's audit program*, (2) *preparing the current year's working papers*, and (3) *assembling the completed case*. It should be noted that the prior year working paper file is purposefully left incomplete to preclude copying and to encourage originality.

New to this edition:

(1) Sarbanes-Oxley materials covering an audit of internal control over financial reporting.
(2) The Introduction includes an overview of an internal control audit and an expanded explanation of how to proceed with an integrated audit.
(3) The Introduction now incorporates an index that cross-references the exhibits to the assignments.
(4) Assignment #1 has been expanded to include a broader analysis of risks in the planning stage of the audit, including an assessment of the risk of material misstatement due to fraud. Also included are requirements for planning an integrated audit of internal control and financial statements.
(5) Risk model exercises have been removed from the assignments and included as an optional exercise in Assignment #4, *Inventory and Purchases*.
(6) Working papers have been created based on the data from the client's computer system to improve the realism of the case.
(7) Optional internal control exercises are based on the client's computer-based LAN system.
(8) The Instructor's CD includes general audit programs that can, at the instructor's discretion, be used as a starting point for students to tailor their audit programs to the client's situation.

I would like to express my appreciation to Linda Chase, Baldwin-Wallace College, for reviewing the entire manuscript and providing helpful suggestions and comments.

Jack W. Paul

Table of Contents

I
General Instructions and Preparations

Peach Blossom Cologne Company
Audit Case

The Peach Blossom Cologne Company audit case illustrates the application of basic auditing principles in a small company audit situation. Auditing Standard 2, *An Audit of Internal Control Over Financial Reporting Performed in Conjunction with an Audit of Financial Statements* requires auditors of public companies to report on their clients' internal control over financial reporting in addition to reporting on the financial statements. This case is designed for familiarization with fundamental audit principles, procedures, and working papers . . . *it by no means exhausts the complexities of a thorough and complete integrated audit of financial statements and internal control over financial reporting*! Because of this design limitation, the case does not include all the procedures required in an actual audit.

INTEGRATED AUDIT PROCESS

An integrated audit of the financial statements and internal control over financial reporting is necessary to infuse both efficiency and effectiveness into the audit process.

Audit of Internal Control Over Financial Reporting

Auditing Standard 2 considerably increases audit requirements and responsibilities.

Management Responsibilities. Public companies are required to include management's report on internal control in the annual report. Specific management responsibilities include:

a. Accepting responsibility for the effectiveness of the company's internal control over financial reporting
b. Evaluating the effectiveness of the company's internal control over financial reporting using suitable control criteria, typically the COSO criteria
c. Supporting its evaluation with sufficient evidence, including documentation; and
d. Presenting a written assessment of the effectiveness of the company's internal control over financial reporting as of the end of the company's most recent fiscal year.

Responsibilities of the External Auditor. The following summarizes the requirements for an audit of internal control over financial reporting:

(i) Set out the terms of the engagement with the client
(ii) Plan the audit
(iii) Evaluate management's assessment of internal control effectiveness
(iv) Obtain an understanding of internal control
(v) Test and evaluate the effectiveness of internal control design
(vi) Test and evaluate the operating effectiveness of internal control
(vii) Formulate an opinion on the effectiveness of internal control over financial reporting
(viii) Obtain management's written representations regarding internal control effectiveness
(ix) Document procedures employed and audit evidence obtained
(x) Issue a report on internal control
(xi) Evaluate management's certification disclosures regarding internal control
(xii) Communicate findings to the audit committee and management.

Although many of these steps are familiar elements of a financial statement audit, an internal control audit requires more extensive procedures and some additional audit steps.[1]

Audit of Financial Statements

Additional procedures to address a *financial statement audit* include:

(1) Establish materiality levels and assess audit risk
(2) Audit the client's business processes and accounts
(3) Evaluate results and issue a report on the financial statements.

Except for issuing the necessary report at the end, where these steps are placed in the foregoing process is a matter of professional judgment. In this audit case, you will not be performing all the steps required to conduct an integrated audit.

WORKING THE ASSIGNMENTS

Problem assignments include the following:

(1) Internal control questionnaire
(2) Instructions and explanations
(3) Evidence to be used during your audit
(4) A form for the audit program listing some of the assertions you will be testing in your work
(5) Client-prepared schedules.

Forms for flowcharting business processes, analyzing control procedures, and assessing control risk are included in Assignment #3, *Accounts Receivable and Credit Sales*, and Assignment #6, *Accounts Payable Processing and Unrecorded Liabilities*. Assignment #4 includes an exercise for computing detection risk. These exercises are optional.

In all assignments, you will be required to obtain an understanding of internal control and prepare a substantive audit program for balances and/or transactions. The financial statement assertions serve as a focal point around which procedures may be grouped to form a program for auditing the financial statements. The assertions are:[2]

(1) **Existence or Occurrence**–the client asserts that assets and liabilities actually exist and that sales and expense transactions actually occurred.

(2) **Completeness**–the client asserts that all transactions and accounts which should be presented in the financial statements are included.

---

[1] For additional information on the internal control audit, see Jack W. Paul, "Exploring PCAOB Auditing Standard 2: Audits of Internal Control," *The CPA Journal*, May 2005.

[2] AICPA Professional Standards, Volume 1 (New York: American Institute of Certified Public Accountants, 2003), AU Sec. 326.03-.08. Copyright 2003 American Institute of Certified Public Accountants, Inc.

(3) **Rights and Obligations**–the client asserts that the company has rights to the assets and that liabilities are the obligations of the company at a given date.

(4) **Valuation or Allocation**–the client asserts that asset, liability, revenue, and expense items have been included in the financial statements at appropriate amounts.

(5) **Presentation and Disclosure**–the client asserts that financial statement components are properly classified, described, and disclosed.

To formulate a program for auditing the financial statements, the auditor first considers the financial statement assertions and then contemplates the audit objectives pertaining to each area. For example consider the assertion, "Accounts receivable exist." For this assertion, the auditor's objective is to obtain and evaluate evidence to verify the existence of the accounts receivable. To achieve this objective, the auditor might send confirmation letters to customers.

ASSESSING AUDIT RISK

Audit risk (AR) is the probability that the auditor unknowingly gives an unqualified opinion when a financial statement assertion is materially in error (for example, the assertion regarding the existence of accounts receivable). Audit risk is composed of three separate risks, defined as follows:[3]

- **Inherent Risk (IR)** - the susceptibility of an assertion to a material misstatement, assuming there are no related internal control structure policies or procedures. Inherent risk can be viewed as the probability that material errors occur in the process leading to the preparation of the financial statements.

- **Control Risk (CR)** - the risk that a material misstatement that could occur in an assertion will not be prevented or detected on a timely basis by an entity's internal control structure policies or procedures. Control risk can be viewed as the probability that, given errors have occurred, internal control does not prevent, detect, or correct those errors.

- **Detection risk (DR)** - the risk that the auditor will not detect a material misstatement that exists in an assertion. Detection risk can be viewed as the probability that the auditor does not detect material errors in the financial statements, given that such errors occur and internal control fails to detect them.

These components can be combined to form the *audit risk model*:

$$AR = IR \times CR \times DR.$$

This model is a tool that provides a starting point for determining the nature (type), extent (quantity), and timing of the audit tests. Audit risk should be set at a relatively low level. Inherent risk is not controllable by the auditor; it must be estimated. Control risk, also not controllable by the auditor, is assessed after analyzing internal control. The auditor can control detection risk only by modifying the

---

[3] See AICPA Professional Standards, Volume 1 (New York: American Institute of Certified Public Accountants, 2003) AU Sec 312A.67. Copyright 2003 American Institute of Certified Public Accountants, Inc.

nature, extent, and/or timing of audit evidence. Thus the auditor can reduce detection risk to an acceptable level by (1) increasing the effectiveness of evidence, that is, changing the *type* of evidence, (2) obtaining *more* evidence, and/or (3) shifting the *timing* of the audit tests closer to the balance sheet date.

For example, assume the auditor is working on accounts receivable. The auditor would like to assure that the risk of material nonexistent accounts does not exceed .05. Accordingly, the desired assurance (confidence) that there are no material fictitious accounts is 95% (1 - .05). Assume that the auditor has assessed inherent risk at .60. This assessment means that the auditor is 40% confident (1 - .60) that material fictitious accounts have not found their way into the client's receivables. We can state that the auditor has 40% confidence in the *nature* of the account. The auditor has assessed control risk at .30. This assessment means that the auditor is 70% (1 - .30) confident that internal control would detect and correct material misstatements of accounts receivable due to nonexistent accounts. On the basis of these inherent and control risk assessments, the detection risk acceptable to the auditor is found to be .28, calculated as follows:

$$DR = \frac{AR}{IR \times CR} = \frac{.05}{.60 \times .30} = .28.$$

What does a detection risk of .28 imply? This is the detection risk acceptable to the auditor in this situation. The auditor has to examine sufficient substantive evidence to reduce the risk of not detecting a fictitious customer account to .28. Consequently, the auditor has to have 72% (1 - .28) confidence in this substantive evidence after the testing has been completed. When this confidence is combined with the confidence obtained from the assessments of the nature of the account (40%) and internal control (70%), the overall audit confidence will be 95%. This is the confidence level obtained from *all* the evidence (including the nature of the account and the controls over it) regarding the presence of material fictitious accounts receivable. The overall audit risk (AR) for this assertion will then be .05.

What would constitute sufficient substantive evidence? With regard to the *nature* of the evidence, the auditor may decide to send confirmation letters. Regarding *extent,* the auditor may elect to confirm only the largest accounts. With respect to *timing*, the auditor may determine that it is not necessary to confirm the receivables at the end of the year. If the acceptable detection risk were *lower* than .28, the auditor would have to obtain *more* evidence to provide more confidence. If the acceptable detection risk were *higher* than .28, the auditor could collect *less* evidence since less confidence would be needed in the substantive testing.

For a variety of reasons, it is not feasible in a case like this to determine the nature, extent, and timing of substantive testing on the basis of inherent and control risk assessments. Nevertheless, the audit risk model provides an *indication* of the degree to which evidence has to be gathered in a specific instance. The model is a convenient *planning tool* and a good *starting point* for specifying substantive testing. Exercises related to the calculation of detection risk are found in Assignment #4, *Inventory and Purchases*. These exercises are *optional*. Your instructor will tell you whether you are to work them.

CONTROL RISK ASSESSMENT

A company's internal control structure consists of five components:

- The control environment

- The company's process for assessing risk
- The information system and business processes related to financial reporting and communication
- Control procedures (or activities)
- The monitoring of controls by the client.

The Control Environment

The control environment provides the auditor with an indication of the effectiveness of the accounting system and control activities. The control environment consists of the following factors:

1. Integrity and ethical values
2. The company's commitment to competence
3. Participation by the board of directors and audit committee
4. Management's philosophy and operating style
5. The company's organizational structure
6. Assignment of authority and responsibility
7. Human resource policies and practices.

The auditor examines each of these factors to assess their impact on control activities and the accounting system.

Control Activities

The optional internal control exercises in Assignments #3 and #6 direct you to list control activities and provide possible tests of those controls. Tests of controls are used to determine whether control policies and procedures are functioning as management has indicated and as documented in the systems narratives and the internal control questionnaires. As you go through the systems narratives (found in the Permanent File materials) and the internal control questionnaires, you should keep in mind six categories of control activities. Use these control categories as a basis for analyzing control strengths and weaknesses and for determining the possible errors and/or irregularities that could occur in each system.

The six categories of control activities consist of two *general control* categories and four *specific control* categories. The general controls provide reasonable assurance that the controls over accounting transactions are functioning properly.

General Controls. Controls providing reasonable assurance that the specific controls are functioning properly:

- **Segregation of functions**–Minimizes incompatible functions.

- **Access to Assets**–Provides proper safeguarding of assets and records by restricting access only to authorized personnel.

In addition to the preceding, general controls in an information technology (IT) environment include such considerations as program controls, logs for monitoring system usage, passwords and data encryption for restricting access to program applications and data, and so on.

Specific (or Application) Controls. Four specific control categories are applicable to monitoring the processing of transactions. Specific controls *follow the flow of transactions* from initiation of the transaction to follow-up. In an IT environment, these types of controls are usually referred to as *application controls*:

- **Authorization**–To assure that transactions are executed in accordance with the specific or general authorization required to engage the company in transactions of the particular type and to ensure that only valid transactions are processed.

- **Input controls**–To assure that all transactions that should be recorded in the accounts are recorded in the correct amounts and are posted to the appropriate accounts. These options imply both *completeness* (the capturing of all transactions) and *accuracy* of data entry (in correct amount and to correct account). Includes numerical sequencing and control of documents, control totals, input edit checks, key verification, check digits, logic tests, holding files, and so on.

- **Processing controls**–To assure that computations affecting the accounts are correctly performed. This category includes, for example, clerical checks, programmed edit tests, logical tests, validity tests, completeness tests, and document matching.

- **Output controls**–Designed to assure that output data are correct. Output controls include reconciliations, user reviews of output and exception reports, and comparison of assets with recorded accountability by means of physical counts.

Tests of Controls

The following tests of controls are typical of those used by auditors to test the design and operating effectiveness of control activities:

(1) **Observation**–Includes observation of control functions and an awareness of events; examples are observation of the safeguarding of assets and the segregation of duties.

(2) **Verbal inquiry**–Involves the collection of oral evidence, for example from management or other client personnel to determine the reasonableness of recorded purchase transactions.

(3) **Vouching**–Examination of documents: following an item backward from a financial record to a supporting document; used, for example, to find approvals on documents or signatures on checks.

(4) **Sequence checking**–Involves examining serially numbered documents to assure that no documents are missing.

(5) **Direct examination**–Includes, for example, the examination of (1) bank reconciliations, (2) sales invoices to determine whether supporting shipping documents are present, (3) minutes for approvals, and (4) the chart of accounts for accuracy.

(6) **Tracing**–The opposite of vouching. Tracing forward through the accounting system from source documents to records, for example to determine whether postings were made.

(7) **Walkthrough**–Consists of selecting a transaction from each major class of transactions and tracing that transaction from authorization and initiation to its reflection in the financial statements. The objectives of a walkthrough are to: (1) corroborate the auditor's understanding of the design of the controls throughout the business process, (2) determine whether all points where misstatements

could occur have been identified, (3) evaluate the design of controls over the business process, and (4) assure that the controls have been placed in operation.

Flowcharting

The following assignments include flowcharting of the following business processes:

Business Process	Assignment
Integration of Accounting System	#1
Sales Revenue and Accounts Receivable Processing	#3
Accounts Payable Processing	#6

If you are directed by your instructor to flowchart these business processes, use flowcharting software and the following symbols:

Document - Input document or output report.

Purchase Order

Journal or Ledger - Designates a journal or ledger.

Sales Journal

Terminal - To show the beginning or end of the flowchart or the receipt or transmittal of information.

From Vendor

Decision - Symbol to indicate that a particular action is required.

Quantity Difference? - No

Yes

Filing Symbol - To show by whom and in what particular manner documents are filed.

By Vendor

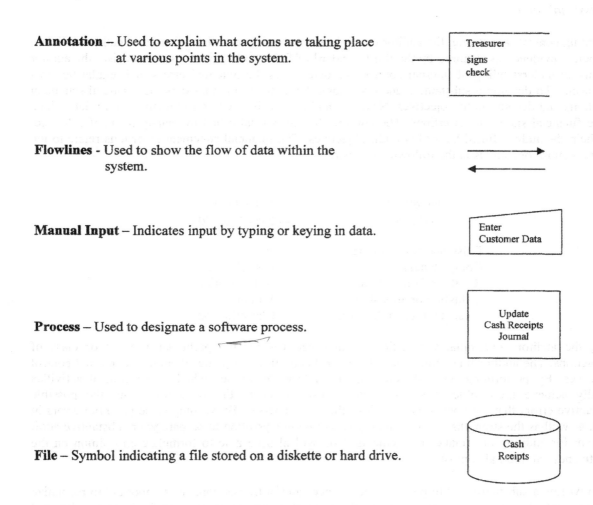

Annotation – Used to explain what actions are taking place at various points in the system.

Treasurer signs check

Flowlines - Used to show the flow of data within the system.

Manual Input – Indicates input by typing or keying in data.

Enter Customer Data

Process – Used to designate a software process.

Update Cash Receipts Journal

File – Symbol indicating a file stored on a diskette or hard drive.

Cash Receipts

In addition to flowcharting, Assignments #3 and #6 contain optional exercises to formally analyze internal control and assess control risk. These optional exercises precede the required substantive exercises. After you have examined the control strengths and weaknesses, you will be in a position to assess control risk and prepare your substantive audit program.

SUBSTANTIVE TESTING

Audit Programs

One of the more important aspects of your auditing course is learning the procedures required for the various audit areas. With this in mind, the starting point for each assignment, other than the optional internal control exercises in Assignments #3 and #6, is the preparation of a substantive audit program for the particular account or group of accounts. You are expected to determine the necessary audit steps from the prior period working papers, the Permanent File materials, internal control questionnaire, problem narrative, the working papers and evidence provided with each problem assignment, and from your textbook. In a real audit situation, the in-charge auditor in the field is responsible for writing an audit program to fit the current year audit engagement. *Placing this responsibility on you in this audit case will increase your ability to assume that decision-making responsibility when you begin your professional career.*

Assuming controls are strong, the auditor can reduce substantive tests that are used to gather sufficient competent evidence as required by the third standard of field work. To assess control risk, the auditor obtains an understanding of internal control and determines the potential errors or irregularities that may occur. To develop a substantive audit program, the auditor first considers the financial statement assertions and devises audit objectives. Next, the auditor specifies control objectives and relates them to the financial statement assertions. The control objectives established by management, if achieved, will help the auditor fulfill his or her audit objectives. The financial statement assertions relate to the general control objectives in the following manner:

Management Assertion	*Related General Control Objective*
Existence or occurrence	Validity
Completeness	Completeness
Rights and obligations	Authorization
Valuation or allocation	Valuation
Presentation and disclosure	Classification

Next, the auditor contemplates specific control objectives for the particular account or class of transactions. The auditor then enumerates the control activities and relates them to the internal control objectives. By performing tests of controls, the auditor determines whether the control activities actually achieve these objectives. The auditor also considers the weaknesses and the possible substantive errors that may occur as a result of these weaknesses. By keeping these potential errors in mind, as well as the strengths in the system, you will be in a position to prepare your substantive audit program for auditing the financial statements. You will also be able to formulate an opinion on the effectiveness of internal control.

When writing a substantive audit program for balances and/or transactions, it is important to recognize management's financial statement assertions, the auditor's audit objectives, and the impact of internal control required to formulate a testable hypothesis. A problem hypothesis is formulated in the manner of a financial statement assertion, such as, "The recorded accounts receivable exist." The auditor begins to write the audit program by explicitly recognizing management's assertions regarding the propriety of the accounting records and amounts. He or she then lists evidence-gathering procedures which, when performed, either support or refute the assertions. Throughout this audit case, whenever you are asked to write a substantive audit program, a few of the assertions typical of that assignment are listed for you. Add other assertions you think are appropriate and then write your program to collect the required evidence.

Substantive Tests

Substantive procedures consist of tests of details of transactions and balances, as well as analytical procedures. Common substantive tests include:

(1) **Recalculation**–The auditor checks calculations performed by client personnel. This is a type of mathematical evidence.

(2) **Physical observation**–This procedure includes the observation of tangible assets and formal documents such as securities and mortgages.

(3) **Confirmation**–Direct correspondence with independent parties.

(4) **Verbal inquiry**–Involves the collection of oral evidence from independent parties and client personnel.

(5) **Vouching**–Examination of documents. Vouching entails following an item from an account backwards through the accounting system to the source documentation that supports the item selected.

(6) **Tracing**–The opposite of vouching. The auditor selects a sample source document and traces forward to verify that the final recording of the item is correct in the journals or ledgers.

(7) **Scanning**–Review of documentation looking for anything unusual in order to identify such items for vouching or tracing.

(8) **Analytical procedures**–The computation and study of financial ratios and amounts. Includes (a) ratio and trend analysis, (b) comparisons with prior years, (c) reference to statistical data produced by independent agencies, and (d) analysis of interrelationships with other data, including related accounts.

PREPARATIONS BEFORE BEGINNING THE ASSIGNMENTS

The administrative office and plant facility of Peach Blossom Cologne Company are located at 1308 Bee Hive Boulevard in Chicago, Illinois. The company is a wholesale distributor of fruit-scented cremes, lotions, oils, colognes, and spray perfumes. More information about the company history and organization is included in the Permanent File materials presented later.

Your auditing firm of Anderson, Olds, and Watershed has performed an annual audit of Peach Blossom Cologne Company since 1995. For the past several years Jasper Parsons, a senior with your firm, performed the audit. Jasper Parsons has left the firm, and you have been assigned as senior auditor in charge of the Peach Blossom Cologne Company audit for the year ended December 31, 2009.

Jasper Parsons completed most of the interim work, including testing of internal control design and operating effectiveness. He also completed the internal control questionnaires with the Controller, Parker Shelton, on December 15, 2009 and updated the internal control narratives at that time. You are to perform your examination in accordance with generally accepted auditing standards and make such tests of the accounting records and perform such other auditing procedures as you consider necessary in the circumstances.

Peach Blossom is a small company and you will be performing all of the audit procedures yourself except where the instructions indicate that an assistant has helped you by performing the audit work on selected accounts. You may assume that the following tasks have been performed in preparation for this audit:

(1) On December 15, 2009, Jasper Parsons completed the internal control questionnaires.

(2) On December 29, 2009, you reviewed prior year's working papers and financial statements of Peach Blossom Cologne Company.

(3) On December 30, 2009, you visited the client's plant and were introduced to the client's personnel. You arranged to have various working paper schedules prepared for you by Don McKenna, an accountant in the controller's office.

(4) On Friday, January 1, 2010, you observed client personnel taking the physical inventory, recorded test counts, and wrote an inventory observation memorandum.

(5) On Monday, January 4, 2010, with the client's assistance, you prepared and mailed all necessary correspondence dealing with confirmations of receivable balances, confirmations of bank balances, cutoff bank statements, accounts and notes payable confirmations, and attorney's letter.

You plan to begin your audit on Monday, January 11, 2010, with an expected completion date of Friday, February 5, 2010. You have received a number of replies from the confirmations, and others will come in as your work proceeds. You have in your possession the various working papers and schedules that Don McKenna prepared for you. In addition, the client's books have been closed for the year, and working trial balances of the balance sheet and income statement accounts have been prepared. You will have last year's audit working papers and the Permanent File on the Peach Blossom Cologne Company.

The current year's trial balance is included in Section IV, which follows immediately after Assignment #8. As you proceed with the audit work, you will find items for which adjusting or correcting entries may be required. *The president of Peach Blossom has stated that he wishes to adjust the company's records for each and every such item you discover, even if immaterial to financial statement presentation.* **Maintain a list of these adjusting entries and post them to working paper AJE (Proposed Adjusting Journal Entries working paper; see this working paper in the prior year's working papers for an example of the proper format). Since each adjustment that you find will be "booked" by the client, post each entry to the current year working trial balance, to the working paper giving rise to the adjustment, and to working paper AJE. Prepare these adjustments as you proceed with the audit.**

As an auditor you are required by PCAOB Auditing Standard 2 to communicate in writing to management and the audit committee of the Board of Directors all *significant deficiencies* and *material weaknesses* in internal control. In addition, you are required to communicate in writing to management all *deficiencies* in internal control. Auditing Standard 2 provides the following definitions:

- *Internal Control Deficiency* – An internal control deficiency exists when the design or operation of a control does not allow management or employees, in the normal course of performing their assigned functions, to prevent or detect **misstatements** on a timely basis.

- *Significant Deficiency* – A control deficiency, or combination of control deficiencies, that adversely affects the company's ability to initiate, authorize, record, process, or report external financial data reliably in accordance with generally accepted accounting principles such that there is *more than a remote likelihood that a* **misstatement** of the company's annual or interim financial statements, **that is *more than inconsequential,*** will not be prevented or detected.

- *Material Weakness* – A significant deficiency, or combination of significant deficiencies, that results in *more than a remote likelihood that a **material misstatement*** of the annual or interim financial statements will not be prevented or detected.

Cognizant of this, you should perform your audit work with the intent of identifying areas of internal control that you consider deficient. When completing the audit (see Assignment #8), preparation of a letter pointing out any material weaknesses, significant deficiencies, or deficiencies and suggesting possible corrective actions is included as an optional exercise. Assignment #8 also includes an exercise for preparing the audit report on internal control over financial reporting.

You may assume that you have read all minutes of stockholder meetings and meetings of the Board of Directors. You have made notes of relevant items from the minutes, and these are included in the Permanent File information. You should cross-reference items of accounting significance that you find in the minutes to appropriate working papers as you prepare them. You should review the Permanent File material (included immediately after these general instructions) before beginning your audit work.

Calendars for two months surrounding the balance sheet date are as follows:

December 2009

SU	MO	TU	WE	TH	FR	SA
		1	2	3	4	5
6	7	8	9	10	11	12
13	14	15	16	17	18	19
20	21	22	23	24	25	26
27	28	29	30	31		

January 2010

SU	MO	TU	WE	TH	FR	SA
					1	2
3	4	5	6	7	8	9
10	11	12	13	14	15	16
17	18	19	20	21	22	23
24	25	26	27	28	29	30
31						

PRIOR YEAR'S WORKING PAPERS

The prior year's working papers are an important resource for completing the current year's audit. The prior year's working papers section is the place to start your work, and you should refer to these working papers often. The prior year's working papers should be used as a starting point for preparing the substantive audit program. They should also be used as a guide for preparing the current year's audit working papers. Please note that the prior year's file includes the basic working papers you will need to complete the audit of the financial statements but does not include all items that would be found in an actual audit situation. You should refer to your textbook to obtain examples of a complete working paper file. Other sources are also available. For example, public accounting firms publish information on working paper files and often make this information available to colleges and universities. Information is also available through the American Institute of Certified Public Accountants (www.aicpa.org).

Turn to the prior year's working papers in Section V. Notice the way the section is laid out, beginning with aggregated information (senior's summary, audit opinions, financial statements, and internal control letter) and moving to the support of this summarized information on the detailed working papers.

Examine the trial balance (TB-BS and TB-IS) prepared by the senior. Notice the form of cross referencing from the supporting working papers. Each significant number on the trial balance is supported by a working paper that documents the accumulation of audit evidence. For example, the accounts payable balances–per books and per audit–on the trial balance are supported by working paper E-1. Turn to this working paper. Notice the tick marks following the suppliers' account balances listed on E-1. These tick marks refer to audit evidence verifying the accuracy of the balance. In addition, notice the cross references to working papers E-3 and E-4. Working papers E-3 and E-4 are confirmations of balances with suppliers. Also notice that working paper E-1 is affected by an audit adjustment that originates on working paper E-2. Examine the cross referencing to the trial balance and the way the adjustment has been set out on working paper E-1 to derive the *balance per audit*.

CURRENT YEAR'S WORKING PAPER FILE

When you begin the audit, set up your current year's working paper file by assembling your working papers in a loose leaf binder. Use the style of working paper cross referencing found in the prior year's working paper file. **In general, each number on a working paper should be supported by a tick mark showing the evidence that corroborates that amount, or to another working paper where the evidence can be found. You should place each audit adjustment you find on: (1) the working paper giving rise to the adjustment, (2) working paper AJE , and (3) the working trial balance.**

Audit programs represent a significant part of the audit as they specify the audit tests to be accomplished. Be very careful when preparing your programs. Set out the specific steps in an understandable fashion. As you go through the audit, cross reference each step in your substantive audit program to the specific weakness in internal control found in the internal control questionnaire (e.g., Q-1, Q-2, etc.).

Assemble your current working papers in the following order:

(1) Senior's Audit Memorandum (from Assignment #8, an optional exercise)
(2) Planning working papers (from Assignment #1)
(3) Draft of audit opinions on the financial statements and internal control (from Assignment #8, optional exercises)
(4) Draft of financial statements and footnotes (from Assignment #8, an optional exercise)
(5) Letter regarding internal control deficiencies and/or material weaknesses (from Assignment #8, an optional exercise)
(6) Working trial balances–balance sheet and income statement
(7) Schedule of adjusting journal entries
(8) Assignment working papers in working paper order (A, B, C, etc.); include internal control analyses (if applicable), and audit program(s) for each assignment with that assignment's working papers.

ELECTRONIC WORKING PAPERS

If you wish to prepare the working papers using spreadsheet software—or if your instructor has directed you to do so—working paper templates are included on the *PBC Working Papers CD*. This CD also includes the time budget worksheet from Assignment #1 and the auditor's trial balances found in Section IV. Use the trial balance file for (1) performing analytical procedures, (2) preparing the financial statements, and (3) performing other computer-based applications as directed by your instructor. The following files are included on *the PBC Working Papers CD* in Excel format:

A-1	Big City National Bank Reconciliation
B-1	Accounts Receivable Aged Trial Balance
C-1	Inventory
C-2	Inventory Observation
D-2	Additions to Property, Plant, and Equipment
D-3	Retirements of Property, Plant, and Equipment
D-4	Depreciation Computation
D-5	Repairs and Maintenance
E-1	Accounts Payable
P-1	Time Budget
TBBS-TBIS	Working Trial Balance

Not all of the working papers are included on this CD. Since letters and confirmations constitute evidence, these documents are to be included as part of your working papers. You should carefully remove these documents from your student book and mark them accordingly with proper working paper headings, indexing, tick marks, and annotations. You should prepare any memoranda using Word, or equivalent. Use Excel to create any working papers that are not included on the CD; the prior year's working papers will serve as a guide.

LIST OF EXHIBITS

The following exhibits are found in the various assignments. These exhibits reflect information pertaining to client documents and records. *Such documents and records belong to the client and are retained by the client.* The auditor uses them as evidence to support the audit opinion.

	Contents of Exhibit	**Assignment**
Exhibit 1	Big City National Bank Cutoff Bank Statement	#2–*Cash*
Exhibit 2	Cash Receipts Journal - December and January (selected portions)	#2–*Cash*
Exhibit 3	Cash Disbursements Journal - December and January (selected portions)	#2–*Cash*
Exhibit 4	Cash Vouchers for Inventory Purchases	#4–*Inventory and Purchases*
Exhibit 5	Cash Vouchers for Property, Plant, and Equipment Disbursements	#5–*Property, Plant, and Equipment*
Exhibit 6	Cash Vouchers for Accounts Payable	#6–*Accounts Payable Processing and Unrecorded Liabilities*
Exhibit 7	Receiving Log for December and January (selected portions) Voucher Register for January (selected portions)	#6–*Accounts Payable Processing and Unrecorded Liabilities*

II
Permanent File
Materials

Peach Blossom Cologne Company
History and Background

The Peach Blossom Cologne Company was founded as a wholesale distributor of scented perfumes in Chicago, Illinois on April 23, 1990. Today, the company handles an expanded line of fruit-scented cremes, lotions, oils, colognes, and spray perfumes. The company purchases large quantities of its products direct from various factory locations. The product is repackaged and distributed to retailers throughout the Chicago metropolitan area and a four-state area extending about 300 miles radially from the plant location.

The company was initially organized in Chicago as a partnership by James Martin and Larry Lancaster. James Martin had been the production manager of a well-known cosmetics manufacturer while Larry Lancaster was a salesman for the same company. Having noticed the role that a wholesaler could play in servicing smaller stores that could not obtain reasonable volume discounts from the larger manufacturers, they started the partnership in 1990, each contributing an equal amount of assets and receiving an equal share of the equity and income distribution. In order to obtain sufficient financing to expand the plant and operations, Martin and Lancaster agreed to incorporate the business in 1997.

The corporation was authorized to issue 20,000 shares of $100 par value common stock. Of the shares authorized, 6,000 were issued; 2,000 each to Martin and Lancaster and 1,000 each to Arthur Broman and Melissa Winchester. Martin and Lancaster took their shares in exchange for their interests in the partnership. Broman and Winchester paid cash for their shares. The capital provided by the sale of stock to Broman and Winchester allowed the company to expand its product lines. This expansion increased sales volume and profitability considerably.

The next stock distribution came in 2001 when 3,250 additional shares were issued. James Martin purchased 2,000 shares of the new issue for cash and the other 1,250 shares were issued for cash in small amounts to ten individuals not previously affiliated with the company. The company's stock is occasionally traded in the over-the-counter market. Peach Blossom is a "small business issuer" as defined by the SEC and is subject to SEC reporting requirements for small businesses that issue securities. As such, Peach Blossom is required to include the auditors' report on internal control over financial reporting in its annual report.

In 1995, the Martin and Lancaster partnership needed to borrow money for working capital. The bank where they applied for the loan required a set of audited financial statements. The CPA firm of Anderson, Olds, and Watershed was engaged by Martin and Lancaster to perform the necessary audit. The audit of Peach Blossom Cologne Company has been a continuing engagement for Anderson, Olds, and Watershed since 1995 and the firm has given an unqualified opinion in each of those years. They also helped with the incorporation procedures in 1997.

Peach Blossom Cologne Company
Organizational Structure

The plant facility is comprised of six major areas: (1) receiving dock, (2) warehouse, (3) repackaging area, (4) shipping dock, (5) garage, and (6) office. A short description of each work area is as follows:

(1) **Receiving dock**–Goods are received directly from the suppliers' factories packaged in cases of 24 units each. Other supply items such as small tools, office supplies, repair parts, and small fixed assets are also received at the receiving dock. A receiving report and receiving log entry are prepared for all materials crossing this dock area.

(2) **Warehouse**–All inventory is held here for repackaging and shipment on customer order. All inventory is stored as received from the factory until a customer order is received.

(3) **Repackaging area**–On customer order, personnel in this area package the shipment according to customer specifications. Sometimes, units (bottles, cans, etc.) can be simply relabeled and shipped as received from the factory. Other orders call for more complex packaging like changing containers and re-labeling.

(4) **Shipping dock**–All materials leaving the plant facility cross this dock and a shipping report is prepared. Inventory shipments to customers comprise nearly all of total shipments.

(5) **Garage**–The company maintains a fleet of automobiles for their salespeople. These cars are serviced from this garage. Forklift tractors used in the repackaging area and delivery vehicles are also serviced and repaired here in the garage.

(6) **Office**–All offices in Peach Blossom Cologne Company are centralized.

Larry Lancaster has overall responsibility for the operation of the company. Louise McWhorter is the president's secretary. Theodore Brown, the production superintendent, has authority over operations of the plant, assisted by the production foreman, Terry Freitag. Under the foreman are three area supervisors; each supervisor employs several hourly paid employees. There are fourteen such hourly employees in all.

Ellen Jacobs is the sales manager; she has a staff of six salaried salespersons. Company salespersons call on Chicago customers at least once a week and out-of-town customers at least once a month. In addition, the office frequently receives calls directly from customers ordering products. Out-of-town customers are supplied with a catalog and frequently call in their orders. The credit manager, Brenda Robertson, coordinates her work between the sales area and the accounting department but reports to Ellen Jacobs. Simon Swift, the accounts receivable clerk, maintains the accounts receivable ledgers and assists Brenda Robertson.

In accounting, the controller, Parker Shelton has a bookkeeper (Donald McKenna) and an accounts payable clerk (Dave Dull). The treasurer's duties are handled by Lillian Stockton assisted by a cashier, Pam Lewis.

The company is organized into five departments (1) administrative, (2) accounting, (3) financial, (4) production, and (5) sales. Information concerning the administrative, accounting, and related financial responsibilities of the various employees of Peach Blossom Cologne Company are as follows:

Each employee's departmental affiliation is designated by the following letter code:

> A–Administrative Department
> C–Accounting Department
> F–Finance Department
> P–Production Department
> S–Sales Department.

PEACH BLOSSOM COLOGNE COMPANY
ADMINISTRATIVE, ACCOUNTING, AND
RELATED FINANCIAL RESPONSIBILITIES

President–Larry Lancaster (A)
1. Reports to Board of Directors
2. Overall authorization

Production Superintendent–Theodore Brown (P)
1. Reports to Larry Lancaster
2. Overall operation of plant

Sales Manager–Ellen Jacobs (S)
1. Reports to Larry Lancaster
2. Overall sales operations
3. Approves all sales orders
4. Supervises six salaried salespersons who prepare sales orders

Controller–Parker Shelton (C)
1. Reports to Larry Lancaster
2. Overall information processing (accounting)
3. Reconciles prelist
4. Signs checks (with treasurer, dual signature)
5. Approves journal entries

Treasurer–Lillian Stockton (F)
1. Reports to Larry Lancaster
2. Overall financial responsibility
3. Controls cash and investments
4. Signs checks (with controller, dual signature)
5. Makes daily bank deposit
6. Reconciles bank account

Secretary to President--Louise McWhorter (A)
1. Reports to Larry Lancaster
2. Corporate secretary
3. Maintains stock certificate book
4. Maintains personnel records and time cards

Bookkeeper--Donald McKenna (C)
1. Reports to Parker Shelton
2. Prepares journal entries and maintains general journal
3. Prepares various other detailed schedules as required
4. Maintains sales register and bills customers
5. Maintains payroll register
6. Maintains general ledger and prepares financial statements

Cashier--Pam Lewis (F)
1. Reports to Lillian Stockton
2. Maintains cash receipts journal
3. Prepares checks for signature
4. Prepares cash deposit

Credit Manager--Brenda Robertson (S)
1. Reports to Ellen Jacobs
2. Approves credit
3. Approves write-offs of delinquent accounts
4. Issues credit memos

Production Foreman--Terry Freitag (P)
1. Reports to Theodore Brown
2. Oversees production
3. Approves purchase orders

Inventory (Storeroom) Clerk--Anita Columbo (P)
1. Reports to Terry Freitag
2. Maintains perpetual inventory records
3. Issues and controls stock at the warehouse

Accounts Receivable Clerk--Simon Swift (S)
1. Reports to Brenda Robertson
2. Maintains accounts receivable subsidiary ledger
3. Prepares cash prelist

Accounts Payable Clerk--Dave Dull (C)
1. Reports to Parker Shelton
2. Maintains accounts payable subsidiary ledger
3. Maintains voucher register (purchases journal)
4. Maintains fixed asset subsidiary ledger
5. Distributes payroll checks
6. Mails checks to vendors

Mailroom Clerk–Gerald Klett (A)
1. Reports to Louise McWhorter
2. Opens mail

Purchasing Agent–Cheryl Palmer (P)
1. Reports to Theodore Brown
2. Makes purchases
3. Prepares purchase orders
4. Maintains vendor invoice and receiving report file
5. Maintains cash disbursements journal

Receiving Dock Manager–William Beauchamp (P)
1. Reports to Terry Freitag
2. Supervises receipt of merchandise
3. Supervises two hourly employees

Repackaging Area Manager–Marsha Doyle (P)
1. Reports to Terry Freitag
2. Overall order preparation
3. Supervises ten hourly employees

Shipping Dock Manager–George Evershock (P)
1. Reports to Terry Freitag
2. Supervises shipping of merchandise
3. Supervises two hourly employees

Peach Blossom Cologne Company
Internal Control

Internal control consists of five components: control environment, risk assessment, control activities, the information (accounting) system and business processes, and monitoring control performance. Information regarding each of these components is provided in this section.

CONTROL ENVIRONMENT

The control environment at Peach Blossom Cologne Company is considered to be good for a small company. Management fosters an atmosphere that enhances the effectiveness of control policies and procedures. Following are comments regarding each of the control environment factors:

(1) **Integrity and Ethical Values**–Our firm has been auditing Peach Blossom Cologne Company for fourteen years. During that time, we have observed only the highest standards of integrity and ethical values among the officers and personnel at Peach Blossom.

(2) **Commitment to Competence**–Management is aware of the need to employ competent people. The various departments carry out training. For the most part, the personnel at Peach Blossom are well trained and competent.

(3) **Board of Directors and Audit Committee Participation**–The Board, especially Larry Lancaster and James Martin, take a keen interest in assuring the proper presentation of financial data. The Audit Committee of the Board of Directors is directly responsible for overseeing the company's financial reporting process on behalf of the Board of Directors. The three members of the Audit Committee are Kevin Chen, Chair, Persephone Fynne, and Roland Mills. These individuals are independent as required by the Sarbanes-Oxley Act of 2002. In addition to their oversight responsibility, the Audit Committee is directly responsible for the appointment, retention, evaluation, and oversight of the work of the independent auditor, including the resolution of disagreements between management and the auditors.

(4) **Management's Philosophy and Operating Style**–Management believes that controls are important. Department heads periodically meet with employees to discuss financial and managerial policies and procedures, including adequate controls.

(5) **Organizational Structure**–Management has not prepared a formal organization chart. Because of the small size of the company, each individual knows his or her duties and responsibilities.

(6) **Assignment of Authority and Responsibility**–Job descriptions are maintained by the personnel manager in a personnel policy manual. In addition, because of the size of the company, each individual is aware of his or her assigned duties. No formal ethical code of conduct has been prepared, but our firm has had no reason to doubt the honesty of management or other employees.

(7) **Human Resource Policies and Practices**–There are no formal training or promotion policies. Hiring, promotion, and dismissal are carried out by the various department heads after consultation with Mr. Lancaster. The Board sets compensation for all salaried personnel. In general, the employees appear to be well-trained and able to perform their respective duties competently.

RISK ASSESSMENT POLICIES

Peach Blossom is a small company. Company officers informally manage risks that may impact financial statement presentation. Monthly budgets are prepared for each department head. These reports are closely scrutinized, exceptions investigated, and explanations obtained for significant variances.

INFORMATION SYSTEM, BUSINESS PROCESSES, AND CONTROL ACTIVITIES

The company's accounting applications are on a local area network (LAN) using software that was purchased from a well-established software vendor. The LAN supports a number of PCs in a multi-user environment. All accounting applications are integrated, but users have access to only specific applications, controlled by means of a user ID and password. Parker Shelton, the controller, administers the LAN and has access to all accounting applications. He controls the passwords and issues them to the various accounting personnel. A user's access to the system is restricted to the specific application(s) needed to carry out the person's duties. Some employees, such as receiving clerks, have access to only specific data elements within a file.

Financial Reporting Cycle–General Ledger Process

Accounts receivable transactions are processed by the accounts receivable clerk, Simon Swift. Cash receipts are maintained by the cashier, Pam Lewis, who also has access to the Accounts Receivable application module. The accounts payable (voucher) register, vendor account balances (accounts payable subsidiary ledger), and the fixed assets are maintained by the accounts payable clerk, Dave Dull. Cash disbursements are maintained by the purchasing agent, Cheryl Palmer. Payroll and sales are maintained by Donald McKenna. Anita Columbo, the inventory storeroom clerk, maintains the inventory records.

The bookkeeper, Donald McKenna, records the journal entries. Parker Shelton, the controller, approves the journal voucher form used to initiate nonrecurring journal entries. After receiving approval, Donald enters the nonrecurring journal entries by keying them into a screen template that immediately performs an online update of the General Ledger Master File. Transactions of a similar nature (accounts payable, cash receipts, sales, and so on) are recorded in the various applications by accounting personnel using the LAN software, which produces daily transaction files (also called transaction registers or special journals), as well as reports detailing the transactions processed by each application. One recurring journal entry is summarized daily from each of these various transaction files. In addition to providing information for decision making, the daily transaction registers and reports serve as an audit trail of transactions that have been processed against the master files in each application.

On a daily basis, Don produces a printout (Daily Listing of Journal Entries) containing the day's recurring journal entries. One recurring journal entry is summarized daily from each transaction file and written onto a Journal Entry Transaction File. This file thus contains daily journal entries, one for each business day, from each of the following accounting applications: Sales Order Entry/Accounts Receivable, Cash Receipts, Accounts Payable, and Cash Disbursements. Don also prints out the transaction registers from these applications and scans them for accuracy. Parker Shelton indicates his approval of the recurring journal entries by initialing the Daily Listing of Journal Entries. After receiving approval, Don processes these recurring entries. The accounting software posts the journal entries from the Journal Entry Transaction File to the General Ledger Master File, thereby updating the general ledger. At the end of the month, Don uses the LAN General Ledger module to prepare the trial balance and financial statements. He then gives these documents to Parker Shelton, who reviews the statements and distributes them to the president and other members of the management team.

Credit Sales System—Sales Order Entry and Accounts Receivable Processing

Customers' orders are received by the sales staff, who enter these orders via a computer screen template into the Sales Order Entry module. This program performs an online update of the Customer Master File and generates a transaction report of sales invoices by customer. (All sales are on credit.) The data in this report are accessed through the LAN by the sales manager, Ellen Jacobs, who prints out the report and indicates approval of each order by initialing the report. The computer software flags those customers whose credit limits are exceeded to preclude the processing of invoices for those customers. The Credit Manager, Brenda Robertson, may override the computer program if, in her judgment, circumstances warrant by annotating the sales invoice transaction report. When Ellen Jacobs and Brenda Robertson are satisfied with the sales orders, they initial the listing. The sales staff enter any necessary corrections and use a menu in the Sales Order Entry module to generate invoices from the Customer Master File. Two-part customer invoices, as well as two copies of a report listing each invoice, are generated and printed. At the time the invoices are processed, the Sales Order Entry module updates the Inventory Master File reducing the on-hand balance in each relevant Inventory Master File record.

One copy of the sales invoice report and the original (top copy) of the sales invoices are sent to Don McKenna, the bookkeeper. Once the items are shipped, Don will mail the original copy to the customers. The second printout of the sales invoice report, along with the second (stock request) copy of the invoices, are sent to the inventory storeroom clerk, Anita Columbo. Anita reviews the invoice listing for errors, such as items that according to the Sales Order Entry system were on hand, but are actually out of stock. Anita accesses the Inventory Master File records and makes corrections for any such discrepancies. She then pulls the ordered items from the shelf and sends the merchandise and the invoices to the repackaging area for filling the customers' orders. (Merchandise is not back ordered; if an item is not in stock, the customer is asked to reorder at a later date.) After marking the quantities on the stock request copy, the repackaging personnel send this copy and the order to shipping. When the order is shipped to the customer, shipping personnel include the stock request copy as a packing slip. The shipping personnel also enter data from the stock request copy into the Sales Order Entry module to produce a shipping report (bill of lading) and update a data field in the Customer Master File indicating that the customer orders were shipped.

At the end of the day, the Sales Order Entry module processes a report of the items that were shipped. Donald McKenna accesses this report and sends the original copy of the invoice to the customer. In addition, the Sales Order Entry module automatically updates the accounts on the Customer Master File for each customer who ordered merchandise. These data are later used by the Accounts Receivable application. At the end of the day, Don prepares a Billed Customer report that serves as the sales register. This report is accessible on the LAN for use by Simon Swift, the accounts receivable clerk. The Accounts Receivable application includes an option allowing Simon to generate a listing of each customer's balance (accounts receivable subsidiary ledger) and a balancing report that provides a reconciliation of the accounts receivable subsidiary ledger to the general ledger accounts receivable control account. Simon Swift prepares a printout of the accounts receivable subsidiary ledger and the balancing report at the end of the day after all sales and cash receipts have been processed. He files these reports daily. The journal entry generated by the Sales Order Entry module is used to update the General Ledger Master File (Accounts Receivable and Sales accounts).

Inventory-Purchases Process

After shipments are processed against the Inventory Master File records (see Credit Sales System procedures), an EOQ (economic order quantity) software routine in the Inventory-Purchases module generates an inventory reorder report, a daily listing of items requiring reorder. Cheryl Palmer, the purchasing agent, uses this report to select items for reorder. Once she has selected the items from the report, Cheryl uses the LAN Inventory-Purchases module to initiate the preparation of a purchase order. The program updates a field in each applicable Vendor Master File record to indicate the items that are on order from each selected vendor. The software also prints purchase orders in three parts, along with a report listing the purchase orders. Each purchase order is signed by the production superintendent, Theodore Brown. Cheryl sends the first copy of the purchase order to the vendor and places the second copy in the Open Purchase Order file pending receipt of the vendor's invoice and the receiving report. Cheryl sends a copy of the purchase order report containing the on-order items to Anita Columbo, the inventory storeroom clerk. Anita is able to access the report data items on the LAN. A menu on the computer screen allows Anita to accept the data in the report and thereby update the "quantity on-order" field in each applicable Inventory Master File record.

The third copy of the purchase order is used as a receiving report. This is a blind copy (no quantities) that is sent to the receiving dock pending receipt of the merchandise. Upon receipt, the material is counted by the receiving clerks, and the quantities received are recorded on the receiving report (third) copy. The receiving personnel enter the receipts into the LAN software, which updates the "merchandise received" field in the applicable Inventory Master File records indicating that the material has been received. The module also prints a daily Receiving Log. The merchandise and the third copy of the purchase order are sent to the warehouse where the merchandise is counted by Anita Columbo. After verifying the receiving clerks' count and reconciling any discrepancies, Anita inputs the inventory count into a computer screen template. The LAN software updates each relevant Inventory Master File record by entering the receiving report number and increasing the quantity on hand. Any differences between the quantity received and the quantity ordered are listed on a report that is sent to Cheryl Palmer along with the third copy of the receiving report. Cheryl accesses this report from the LAN and uses it to reconcile any differences with the vendor.

Accounts Payable Process

Upon receipt of the invoice from the vendor and the receiving report from the storeroom clerk, Cheryl Palmer matches these documents with the second copy of the purchase order. Cheryl sends all three documents to the accounts payable clerk, Dave Dull, who uses a menu in the Accounts Payable module to initiate an update of the Vendor Master File records; this routine computes the new balance due each vendor. The software also updates the Inventory Master File records by multiplying the new vendor inventory cost times the quantity on hand (that was entered by Anita Columbo) to yield a new inventory value. In addition, the software module prints a covering payment voucher for each vendor and produces a voucher register report listing the vouchers. After obtaining the controller's signature on each voucher, the voucher package (covering voucher, invoice, and supporting documentation) is then filed in the unpaid bills file by due date. (Any voucher not approved is backed out.) The journal entry generated by the Accounts Payable module is used to update the General Ledger Master File (Accounts Payable and Inventory accounts).

On a daily basis, Dave accesses a menu in the program to produce an updated accounts payable subsidiary ledger report indicating the current balance due each vendor. After the general ledger is posted, the routine produces a balancing report reconciling the subsidiary ledger to the Accounts Payable control account.

As vouchers are processed, the payment date in the Vendor Master File triggers the software to print a daily Cash Requirements report that lists those vouchers requiring payment. Dave removes those voucher packages from the unpaid bills file and sends them, along with the supporting documentation and the Cash Requirements report, to Cheryl Palmer. After verifying that the check amounts are correct by referencing the voucher and supporting documentation, Cheryl uses the Cash Requirements report and a menu in the Cash Disbursements module to initiate the preparation and printing of the checks. The software program also produces a listing of the checks. This listing is used to generate the daily cash disbursements journal (register). The Cash Disbursements module also generates a daily journal entry that is used to update the General Ledger Master File (Accounts Payable and Cash accounts).

The voucher packages, checks, and a printout of the detailed amounts from the cash disbursements update process are forwarded to the treasurer, Lillian Stockton, who reviews the invoices and other documentation and signs the checks, along with the controller. The treasurer cancels the documents by stamping them "Paid" and sends the checks and canceled voucher packages to Dave Dull, who mails the checks to the vendors and files the canceled voucher packages.

MONITORING INTERNAL CONTROL PERFORMANCE

Management uses the COSO framework as the criteria for evaluating the effectiveness of internal control over financial reporting. The company does not have an internal audit department but has selected competent personnel from each area impacting financial reporting. These individuals periodically conduct evaluations of internal control effectiveness including the documentation of controls, as well as the testing of design and operating effectiveness and documentation of the test results.

Peach Blossom Cologne Company
Chart of Accounts

Each account number in the company's chart of accounts is a three-digit number. The first digit in the number is a code digit that identifies the nature of the account. The following is a listing of each code digit shown with the type of account it identifies.

1--Current assets
2--Long-term assets
3--Current liabilities
4--Long-term liabilities
5--Capital stock and other
   contributed capital

6--Retained earnings and dividends
7--Revenues from operations
8--Expenses of operations
9--Nonoperating revenues and expenses

List of Account Numbers

101--Cash--Big City National Bank
105--Accounts Receivable
106--Allowance for Bad Debts
107--Miscellaneous Receivables
109--Inventory

210--Land
220--Buildings
221--Accumulated Depreciation, Buildings
230--Machinery and Equipment
231--Accumulated Depreciation, Machinery
   and Equipment
240--Automotive Equipment
241--Accumulated Depreciation,
   Automotive Equipment
250--Office Furniture and Fixtures
251--Accumulated Depreciation, Office
   Furniture and Fixtures

301--Accounts Payable
305--Accrued Interest
306--Dividends Payable
307--Federal Income Taxes Payable
308--Notes Payable--Short Term

401--Notes Payable--Long Term

501--Common Stock
505--Other Contributed Capital

601--Retained Earnings

605--Dividends
610--Income Summary (Current Net Income)

701--Sales
703--Sales Returns and Allowances

801--Cost of Goods Sold
820--Wage and Salary Expense
821--Payroll Tax Expense
822--Depreciation Expense
823--Rent Expense
824--Office Supplies Expense
825--Small Tools Expense
826--Advertising Expense
827--Insurance Expense
828--Repairs and Maintenance
829--Property Taxes Expense
830--Utilities Expense
831--Professional Fees
832--Miscellaneous Expense
833--Provision for Bad Debts
834--Freight-out Expense

901--Interest Expense
930--Gain/Loss on Sales of Fixed Assets
940--Federal Income Tax Expense
950--Miscellaneous Income and Adjustments

Regular Meeting, January 7, 2008:
- No business of audit significance.

Regular Meeting, February 15, 2008:
- Approved 2007 annual report and authorized its release to stockholders.

Annual Meeting, February 29, 2008:
- Elected officers and approved salaries for 2008.

Chairman of the Board	Mr. James Martin	No Salary
President	Mr. Larry Lancaster	$90,700
Secretary	Ms. Louise McWhorter	25,200
Other Board Members	Mr. Arthur Broman	No Salary
	Mr. Kevin Chen, Audit Committee Chair	No Salary
	Ms. Persephone Fynne	No Salary
	Mr. Roland Mills	No salary
	Ms. Melissa Winchester	No Salary

Other salaries and wages were approved for 2008 as follows:

Theodore Brown, Production Superintendent	$64,800
Terry Freitag, Production	43,200
Cheryl Palmer, Purchasing Agent	36,000
William Beauchamp, Receiving Dock Manager	36,000
Marsha Doyle, Repackaging Area Manager	36,000
George Evershock, Shipping Dock Manager	36,000
Anita Columbo , Inventory Clerk	23,000
Ellen Jacobs, Sales Manager	46,000
Salespersons (4)	43,200
Brenda Robertson, Credit Manager	32,000
Simon Swift, Accounts Receivable Clerk	23,200
Parker Shelton, Controller	39,600
Donald McKenna, Bookkeeper	28,300
Dave Wilson, Accounts Payable Clerk	25,000
Lillian Stockton, Treasurer	39,600
Pam Lewis, Cashier	23,000
Gerald Klett, Mail Clerk	21,000

Nonsalaried positions were approved at various hourly rates.

- Appointed the law firm of Edwards, Overstreet, and Gilley as General Counsel for the year 2008.

- Appointed the CPA firm of Anderson, Olds, and Watershed as auditors for the year 2008.

- Approved construction of a garage and maintenance shop for the automotive fleet. Awarded the job to Taggart Construction Company on a bid of $33,500. (D-2)

- Approved the disposal of the lot located at 1212 Westminster Road. (D-3)

Regular meeting, April 4, 2008:
- Authorized Ms. Stockton to engage in short term borrowings of up to $120,000 as needed and to negotiate a loan of $125,000 with the Big City National Bank. Proceeds of the loans are to be used for operations and to enter the nonflourocarbon aerosol and the pump spray markets if the results of a feasibility study prove favorable. (F-1)

Regular meeting, May 2, 2008:
- Approved purchase of used 2005 Ford Focus, $9,300. (D-2)

- Approved purchase of four used Delta computers at $1,095 each. (D-2)

- Approved purchase of eight Kardex filing cabinets at $284.75 each. (D-2)

Regular meeting, July 11, 2008:
- No business of audit significance.

Regular meeting, August 8, 2008.
- No business of audit significance.

Regular meeting, September 5, 2008:
- No business of audit significance.

Regular meeting, October 3, 2008:
- Approved purchase of Atwell-Henley Box Folding machine, $5,045. (D-2)

Regular meeting, November 7, 2008:
- Declined sales department request for three new automobiles.

Regular meeting, December 5, 2008:
- Authorized payment of annual dividend of $15,725 on January 19, 2009 to common shareholders of record on December 31, 2008. (H-1)

- Authorized Ms. Jacobs to hire two more salespersons due to increased advertising campaign and sales program.

Regular meeting, January 9, 2009:
- No business of audit significance.

Regular meeting, January 9, 2009:
o   No business of audit significance.

Regular meeting, February 13, 2009:
o   Approved 2008 annual report and authorized its release to stockholders.

Annual meeting, February 27, 2009:
o   Elected officers and approved salaries for 2009:

Chairman of the Board	Mr. James Martin	No Salary
President	Mr. Larry Lancaster	$95,100
Secretary	Ms. Louise McWhorter	26,400
Other Board Members	Mr. Arthur Broman	No Salary
	Mr. Kevin Chen, Audit Committee Chair	No Salary
	Ms. Persephone Fynne	No Salary
	Mr. Roland Mills	No Salary
	Ms. Melissa Winchester	No Salary

Other salaries and wages were approved for 2009 as follows:

Theodore Brown, Production Superintendent	$67,900
Terry Freitag, Production Manager	45,300
Cheryl Palmer, Purchasing Agent	37,750
William Beauchamp, Receiving Dock Manager	37,750
Marsha Doyle, Repackaging Area Manager	37,750
George Evershock, Shipping Dock Manager	37,750
Anita Columbo, Inventory Clerk	24,100
Ellen Jacobs, Sales Manager	48,300
Salespersons (6)	45,300
Brenda Robertson, Credit Manager	33,500
Simon Swift, Accounts Receivable Clerk	24,300
Parker Shelton, Controller	41,500
Donald McKenna, Bookkeeper	29,600
Dave Dull, Accounts Payable Clerk	22,500
Lillian Stockton, Treasurer	41,500
Pam Lewis, Cashier	24,100
Gerald Klett, Mail Clerk	22,000

Nonsalaried positions were approved at various hourly rates.

o   Appointed the law firm of Edwards, Overstreet, and Gilley as General Counsel
    for the year 2009.
o   Appointed the CPA firm of Anderson, Olds, Watershed as auditors for the
    year 2009.

Regular meeting, April 3, 2009:
o   Approved the disposal of a forklift that was severely damaged after falling off the receiving dock. Due to its age, there would be no insurance reimbursement. Mr. Freitag was asked to seek the best means of disposing of the asset.
o   Authorized Ms. Stockton to negotiate a $150,000 loan with the Midwestern Mutual Life Insurance Company for 10 years at 10 1/2%. The loan will be used to finance a new overhead storage and retrieval system for the warehouse. Plant machinery and equipment will be pledged as collateral.

Regular meeting, May 1, 2009:
o   Approved the purchase of a new forklift tractor at a cost of $18,900 to replace the one that was damaged last month.

Regular meeting, June 5, 2009.
o   Approved installation of a warehouse overhead storage and retrieval system. Awarded contract to Thompson Industrial Systems for their $178,200 bid.

Regular meeting, July 10, 2009:
o   No business of audit significance.

Regular meeting, August 7, 2009:
o   Approved the purchase of a package labeling machine from Simon-Weller Manufacturing Co. at a cost of $8,400.

Regular meeting, September 4, 2009.
o   Approved purchase of two Itsubitsi photocopiers at $3,400 each: $6,800.

Regular meeting, October 2, 2009:
o   Approved feasibility study introduced by Mr. Brown regarding expansion into the nonfluorocarbon aerosol spray market. Mr. Brown explained that the firm of Kalvin and Hubbs Consulting would provide Peach Blossom with recommendations as to whether to proceed or to abandon the project. Mr. Brown noted that Kalvin and Hubbs would complete the study by the end of December, 2009. This schedule would provide time to begin purchasing equipment in April, 2010 for entry into the market by the end of 2010 if the project proves feasible.

Regular meeting, November 6, 2009:
o   Approved purchase of a Ford sedan, $19,500.

Regular meeting, December 4, 2009:
o   Authorized payment of annual dividend of $15,725 on January 25, 2010 to common shareholders of record on December 31, 2009.

Regular meeting, January 8, 2010:
o   Authorized Mr. Freitag to negotiate a contract with the McWilliams Vending and Supply Company whereby the latter would install and service food and drink vending machines in the employees' lunchroom.
o   Authorized Mr. Brown and Ms. Jacobs to solicit three bids for the purchase of a 4-passenger airplane for use by company management and sales personnel.

III
Problem Assignments

Assignment #1
Planning the Integrated Audit

The first standard of field work requires that the audit work be adequately planned. Other standards stipulate that the auditor is to obtain an understanding of the internal control structure, including the control environment, procedures for assessing risks, control activities, the information system, and the company's processes for assessing the quality of internal control performance.[1] The objective of your integrated audit of Peach Blossom's financial statements and internal control over financial reporting is to be able to provide an opinion on both. To familiarize yourself with Peach Blossom Cologne Company and to devise an overall audit strategy for the conduct of your integrated audit, you have decided to develop a formal audit plan. In order to devise this plan, study the Permanent File Materials, including the following sections: *History and Background, Organizational Structure,* the *Internal Control* section.

The following questionnaires dealing with the control environment and the administration of the local area network (LAN) were prepared by the audit senior, Jasper Parsons, on December 15, 2009. To further your understanding of Peach Blossom's control environment, you should study the questionnaires and contemplate the implications of questions that are answered "no." You should keep these items in mind as you carry out your audit procedures.

Internal Control Questionnaire–Control Environment

		Yes	*No*	*Comments*
1.	Does management demonstrate a prudent attitude toward business risk, including an honest and sensible approach to financial reporting and meeting profits and financial goals?	√	__	_____
2.	Has the client prepared an organization chart?	__	√	_____
3.	Is there an Audit Committee of the board of directors?	√	__	_____
4.	Are lines of authority and the means of assigning responsibility clearly spelled out?	√	__	_____

5. Are procedures sufficient to provide management

---

[1] Auditing standards also require the auditor to plan and perform the audit to obtain reasonable assurance that the financial statements are free of material misstatement due to fraud. See SAS 99 for specific requirements.

with the ability to control the performance of company employees and effectively supervise company activities? √ ___ *Peach Blossom is small enough that managers are able to maintain good control.*

6. Is a budget prepared for control purposes, showing variances from planned performance? √ ___

7. Are accounting and control procedures documented? √ ___

8. Does the client maintain a chart of accounts? √ ___

9. Are financial statements prepared periodically for submission to management? √ ___

                       Monthly

10. Are journal entries approved by a responsible official? √ ___

                       By controller who initials them.

11. Is there an internal audit function? ___ √

12. Are personnel policies and practices adequate to ensure that competent employees are hired, that employees are trained, periodically evaluated, and adequately compensated for the responsibilities assigned? √ ___

13. Are employees provided the resources to enable them to carry out their assigned duties? √ ___

14. Are all personnel who have financial responsibilities required to take annual vacations? ___ √

15. Are employees who handle cash or similar assets bonded? √ ___

Internal Control Questionnaire–LAN General Controls

		Yes	No	Comments
1.	Is there a designated LAN administrator?	√	___	*Parker Shelton, the controller, performs this function.*
2.	Are system administration and operations procedures documented?	√	___	
3.	Are users precluded from accessing or changing				*The LAN uses purchased*

LAN program source code?

√   __   *software; program source code is not accessible to users.*

4. Is a standard form used to document requests for the addition, change, or deletion of LAN access capabilities?

√   __   _____

5. Are group or shared user IDs prohibited?

√   __   _____

6. Are access privileges granted to LAN user's on a need-to-know basis?

√   __   *User access is restricted to the specific application needed for his or her function.*

7. Are output devices in a secure area that limits access only to those authorized?

__   √   *The printers are available to anyone. LAN reports are left unlocked.*

8. Is the LAN server secured from unauthorized individuals?

√   __   _____

9. Is critical equipment protected from theft?

√   __   _____

10. Is virus checking software in use?

√   __   _____

11. Is there a complete documentation of all files associated with the LAN system?

√   __   _____

12. Are backup and recovery procedures documented?

√   __   _____

13. Are critical files identified and backed-up?

√   __   _____

14. Are backup files stored off-site?

√   __   _____

15. Are users prohibited from using unlicensed software or software downloaded from unofficial sources?

√   __   _____

16. Is a list of licensed software maintained for the LAN?

√   __   _____

Materiality

For planning purposes, your firm uses 5% of pretax income as a materiality level for determining whether the financial statements require adjustment. **The president of Peach Blossom has asked you to record all items you find requiring adjustment even if they are not considered to be material. You should therefore post all adjustments you find for inclusion in the financial statements. Nevertheless, you should use the 5% of pretax income amount as a materiality reference point for planning the scope of the audit.**

Audit Planning Exercises

Complete those exercises below that have been assigned by your instructor.

1. Engagement Letter

The audit engagement letter is an important document that sets out the understanding between the client and the audit firm. While reviewing the Peach Blossom engagement file after Jasper Parson's departure, the partner in charge of the Peach Blossom audit discovered that Jasper had not obtained a signed engagement letter for the current year's audit. Since the engagement letter sets out the terms of the contract between the audit firm and the client, the engagement partner is quite anxious to obtain the signed letter before you begin your audit field work. Consequently, she has asked you to prepare an engagement letter for the Peach Blossom audit.

Required. Read Part I, *General Instructions and Preparations*, and Part II, *Permanent File Materials*. Prepare an engagement letter in good form addressing it to Mr. Kevin Chen, Chair of the Audit Committee of the Board of Directors. Your letter should contain the following elements:

- A list of the specific services to be rendered by the firm.
- An explanation of the nature of an integrated audit engagement, as well as its limitations.
- A statement that the firm will evaluate internal control and will prepare a written communication regarding all internal control deficiencies, significant deficiencies, and material weaknesses discovered.
- The expected audit completion date.
- A statement to the effect that assistance will be required from client personnel.
- A statement to the effect that the completion date may have to be extended if unforeseen circumstances arise.
- A statement that the firm cannot be expected to discover all fraudulent acts or other irregularities.
- An indication of the basis for the fee, i.e., that the fee is based on time expended and may increase from the initial estimate if unusual circumstances are encountered.

Date the letter December 18, 2009 and sign the firm's name: Anderson, Olds, and Watershed. The letter should have a space for the signature of the person who accepts the terms of the engagement on behalf of Peach Blossom Cologne Company. This is the chair of the Audit Committee of the Board, Mr. Kevin Chen. There should also be a space for this person's title, as well as the date accepted. *Use word processing software.*

2. Time Budget

Despite having completed most of the interim work, Jasper Parsons left without preparing a time budget for the audit. The partner in charge has asked you to prepare this budget for the current year's engagement. Form P-1 has the actual hours expended in the previous year. Last year the auditors attempted to save time by cutting the hours allotted for planning and interim work. As a consequence, the audit team had to perform additional year-end work and expended a great deal of overtime due to unforeseen circumstances. These eventualities could likely have been avoided had the team spent more time during planning, and at interim. The partner-in-charge would like to reduce the total time for this year's audit to 200 hours while avoiding the pitfalls encountered in the previous year. She believes this is possible if certain modifications are made. Specifically, planning should be increased to approximately 10-15% of total budgeted hours. Time spent during the interim period should be augmented to total approximately 30% of the budgeted hours, while supervision and review time should be approximately

20% of the total hours. You may assume that most of the interim work related to testing controls for the internal control audit has been completed. Regarding personnel, you (the in-charge senior) will complete the interim work and perform the bulk of the year-end work. You will be assisted by an assistant staff auditor during certain phases of the engagement. Specifically, with regard to the year-end work, an assistant will: (1) perform work on operating (income statement) accounts, (2) tally the trial balance, (3) take excerpts from minutes and correspondence, (4) perform detailed work in the area of unrecorded liabilities, and (5) complete any additional testing of internal control.

Required. Prepare the time budget for this year's audit by completing the *Current Year Budget* and *Percent* columns on form P-1. For those who prefer to work with spreadsheet software, use the time budget file on the PBC Working Papers CD. (Hint: As a way of assessing the relative amount of time to be spent on each audit area, examine the current year's working trial balance. Keep in mind that certain accounts in a merchandising company are usually significant and typically present more audit risk. These accounts include Inventory, Accounts Receivable, and Accounts Payable. Those accounts, as well as other larger, more material accounts appearing on the trial balance should be assigned a relatively greater proportion of the budgeted time. You should also use the prior year's working papers to guide your allocation of hours for this year's audit.)

3. **Organization Chart**
   Peach Blossom has not prepared a formal organization chart.

   Required.
   (a) Prepare an organization chart for the company. Use the information concerning administrative, accounting, and related financial responsibilities, found in the *Organizational Structure* section of the casebook, as well as other information in the Permanent File Materials. Start with the Board of Directors. Prepare the organization chart on form P-2, or use software and label the chart P-2.
   (b) In a separate narrative, describe any organizational changes that would improve internal control.

4. **Flowchart of Financial Reporting Cycle**
   Read the narrative describing the Financial Reporting Cycle under *Information System, Business Processes, and Control Activities* found in the Internal Control section of the Permanent File Materials.

   Required. Prepare a flowchart of the Financial Reporting Cycle using the captions provided on form P-3. These captions identify Peach Blossom's business processes and the more important accounts associated with them. Show the flow of transactions from each LAN application module to the preparation of the posting to the general ledger, preparation of the financial statements, and distribution of the statements. For this flowchart, start with the transaction file (register) associated with each application; show the flow to the Journal Entry Transaction file and the daily updating of the General Ledger Master file, as well as the monthly preparation and distribution of the financial statements. Prepare the flowchart using *flowcharting software,* such as PowerPoint.

5. **Analytical Procedures and Risk Analysis**
   In order to obtain valuable information to aid in the planning effort, the auditor performs analytical procedures. Analytical procedures are used in the initial planning stages to identify matters that may require attention during the audit. Accordingly, these procedures help determine the nature, extent, and timing of audit testing. Some of the more common analytical procedures conducted during the planning phase are (1) comparison of current period financial data with those of prior periods, (2) analysis of financial ratios, and (3) examination of the interrelationships of financial and nonfinancial information.

   The 2008 and 2009 trial balances file is found on the PBC Working Papers CD.

Required. Perform the following analytical procedures in order to gather valuable planning information. Use *spreadsheet software*, and be sure to turn in a printout of your work:

(a) *Change Analysis.* Calculate the dollar and percentage increase or decrease in the various balance sheet and income statement account balances between the fiscal years ended 2008 and 2009. Use the following column headings:

Per Audit 12-31-08	Per Books 12-31-09	Dollar Change	Percent Change

Index your spreadsheet working paper PL-1.

(b) *Common Size Financial Statements.* From the figures found on the income statement working trial balance, calculate sales returns and expense accounts as a percentage of gross sales for the years 2008 and 2009. Use the following four column headings:

Per Audit 2008	2008 Percent of Gross Sales	Per Books 2009	2009 Percent of Gross Sales

Index your spreadsheet working paper PL-2.

(c) *Financial Ratios.* Calculate the following financial ratios to reveal any problem areas and be in a position to assess the financial condition of the company.[2] (Note that net credit sales = net sales.):

Ratio	**Formula**
Liquidity Ratios	
(1) Current ratio	$\dfrac{\text{current assets}}{\text{current liabilities}}$
(2) Quick ratio	$\dfrac{\text{cash} + \text{net trade accounts receivable} + \text{marketable securities}}{\text{current liabilities}}$
Activity Ratios	
(3) Accounts receivable turnover	$\dfrac{\text{net credit sales}}{\text{net trade accounts receivable}}$
(4) Days' receivables	$\dfrac{365}{\text{accounts receivable turnover}}$
(5) Inventory turnover	$\dfrac{\text{cost of goods sold}}{\text{inventory}}$

---

[2]The formulas used in these ratios comply with those found in the major financial services that report industry statistics.

(6)   Days' inventory

$$\frac{365}{\text{inventory turnover}}$$

(7)   Asset turnover

$$\frac{\text{net credit sales}}{\text{total assets}}$$

Profitability Ratios

(8)   Income to net worth

$$\frac{\text{net income (after taxes)}}{\text{assets - liabilities}}$$

(9)   Income to total assets

$$\frac{\text{net income (after taxes)}}{\text{total assets}}$$

Leverage Ratios

(10)   Liabilities to net worth

$$\frac{\text{total liabilities}}{\text{assets - liabilities}}$$

(11)   Liabilities to total assets

$$\frac{\text{total liabilities}}{\text{total assets}}$$

(12)   Times interest earned

$$\frac{\text{net after tax income + interest expense + income taxes}}{\text{interest expense}}$$

You have obtained the following median industry ratios for analyzing the results:

Ratio	Median Industry Ratio
Current	1.90
Quick	.90
Accounts receivable turnover	10.43
Days' receivables	35.00
Inventory turnover	5.85
Days' inventory	62.39
Asset turnover	2.83
Income to net worth	.12
Income to total assets	.05
Liabilities to net worth	1.11
Liabilities to total assets	.53
Times interest earned	3.00

Calculate the ratios on a separate part of the worksheet. Set up the formulas, entering the correct spreadsheet cells. Use the following headings:

Ratio	2008	2009	Median Industry

Index your spreadsheet working paper PL-3.

(d) *Analytical Procedures Memorandum.* Having carried out these analytical procedures, prepare a memorandum to assess the implications for your upcoming audit of Peach Blossom Cologne Company. *Use word processing software.* Include the following in your memorandum:

(1) *An Analysis of Audit Risks.* Relying on the results of the change analysis obtained in Requirements (a) and (b) above, list the accounts that appear to require attention because of significant changes. Establish and state your decision threshold for selecting accounts to be flagged for further examination. For example, you may decide to seek explanations for changes exceeding 20% or $5,000. For each such account that you identify, provide two plausible reasons for the fluctuation in the account: (1) first, a logical and reasonable business (operational) reason; (2) second, a possible client error (or irregularity) that may have caused the account to be misstated. In making these determinations, you should review the prior period working papers, as well as the Permanent File materials. For example, if the balance of accounts receivable is significantly higher in the current year than in the previous year, an obvious business reason is that sales have increased. A possible client error is inclusion of January sales in December. In this situation, the auditor's concern is that sales were not recorded in the correct time period. The possible effect of this error is overstatement of Sales Revenue on the income statement and Accounts Receivable on the balance sheet. (Hint: refer to on your audit text for the types of errors that may affect the various accounts.)

(2) *Analysis of Questionable Accounts.* Discuss other accounts that may appear questionable, for example accounts that do not change when a change is expected.

(3) *Assessment of the Risk of Financial Failure.* Audit clients that are experiencing operational problems or are near bankruptcy can present significant audit problems. If sales are declining or growth has slowed, management may be inclined to manipulate the financial records. For such reasons, the auditor needs to assess the client's financial status. *Assess the financial condition of Peach Blossom Cologne Company and the consequent audit risk related to client financial failure.* Rely on the financial ratio analysis from Requirement (c), as well as any other information you have at hand. Refer to your finance text and other resources to determine the meaning of each of these ratios. Whenever possible, relate the ratio analysis to the change analysis in Requirements (a) and (b). For example, if inventory turnover has slowed, relate this fact to any change in inventory.

(4) *Overall Appraisal of Audit Risk.* Provide an overall assessment of the audit risk associated with this engagement. Base this assessment on the analytical procedures you have performed and the knowledge of the client you gleaned from the Permanent File Materials. Assess whether Peach Blossom is a *low, moderate,* or *high* risk audit client. In making this determination, consider the likelihood of bankruptcy, the integrity of management, the state of the client's internal controls, the likelihood of audit failure, and the probability of litigation stemming from this audit engagement. Explain your conclusions.

6. Assessing the Risk of Material Misstatement Due to Fraud

According to generally accepted auditing standards the auditor is explicitly required to assess the risk of material misstatement in the financial statements due to fraud and is required to consider this assessment when specifying the procedures to be performed during the audit. The auditor is required to consider two types of misstatements: (1) those arising from fraudulent financial reporting, and (2) misstatements brought about by the misappropriation of assets.

Required:

Read SAS 99, *Consideration of Fraud in a Financial Statement Audit,* paying special attention to the appendix, which provides numerous examples of fraud risk factors. Next read the Permanent File materials (Section II) and the internal control questionnaires in Assignments 1 through 7. Based on the permanent file materials and the questionnaires, identify each factor that may impact the risk of fraud in the Peach Blossom Cologne Company audit as far as you can determine. For each factor that you so identify, comment on (1) why this factor may have a significant impact on the risk of fraud in this audit, and (2) the evidence and actions required to reduce the risk.

7. **Internal Control Over Financial Reporting: Planning Memorandum**

Review your auditing textbook, articles dealing with audits of internal control over financial reporting,[3] and Auditing Standard 2.

Required. Prepare a memorandum describing how your audit firm, Anderson, Olds and Watershed, plans to conduct the audit of internal control. Date your memorandum the start of the fiscal year under audit, January 1, 2009. Include the following points:

(1) How the firm will evaluate management's process for assessing the effectiveness of Peach Blossom's internal control.
(2) How Peach Blossom's internal control design and operating effectiveness should be tested.
(3) The *timing* and *extent* of internal control testing required to provide an audit opinion on internal control over financial reporting.
(4) The use of work performed by client personnel.
(5) The procedures the firm will use to evaluate weaknesses in internal control including differentiating among deficiencies, significant deficiencies, and material weaknesses.
(6) Enumerate the different parts of the unqualified opinion on internal control over financial reporting. Explain the meaning of each part.

8. **Audit Planning Memorandum**

Required. Read the *General Instructions and Preparations* and the *Permanent File Materials*. Prepare a formal planning memorandum for the audit partner describing (a) each of the matters that should be considered in planning an audit (listed below as items 1-13) and (b) a description of the procedures you have carried out, or will carry out, in planning the engagement (items 14-18). Include in your memorandum a conclusion regarding the relative level of risk involved in this audit engagement. Date your memorandum December 28, 2009; assume that the December 31, 2009 trial balance is available to you. (For purposes of this memorandum, you should not include the details of specific business processes or their controls.) *Use word processing software.*

Concerning the matters to consider when planning the audit, discuss the following items in your memorandum:
(1) the objective of your integrated audit (What is the ultimate goal?)
(2) the timing and staffing of the engagement (see Exercise 2, Time Budget)
(3) the company's pertinent aggregate financial data (e.g., Total Assets)

---

[3] For example, see Jack W. Paul, "Exploring PCAOB Auditing Standard 2: Audits of Internal Control," *The CPA Journal*, May 2005.

(4) the history and background of the company

(5) the principals (owners) and their qualifications

(6) the integrity of client management

(7) the state or condition of the company's internal control over financial reporting

(8) capitalization (i.e., percentage of assets financed by debt and percentage financed by equity)

(9) the type of company (public/nonpublic) and reporting requirements

(10) the markets served

(11) materiality level for planning the audit work (use 5% of pretax income)

(12) likely audit adjustments, especially those affecting net income (see prior year's working papers)

(13) the type of opinions you expect to render on the financial statements and on internal control over financial reporting.

As to the procedures you will carry out, briefly discuss the following matters:

(14) how you will familiarize yourself with the company and the industry (internet resources, trade journals, etc.)

(15) what you will do regarding outsiders rendering services (e.g., attorneys)

(16) schedule of the major audit work yet to be completed—when work will be performed, e.g., inventory observation—see prior year's working papers (Assume that interim work on internal control over financial reporting, as well as various accounts and business processes, has already been performed by Jasper Parsons and assistants under his supervision.)

(17) the scope and timing of audit work (if any) to be performed by the client's staff (Hint: What work did the client's staff perform during the previous audit?)

(18) the probable audit report date (see prior year's working papers).

Peach Blossom Cologne Company
Time Budget
December 31, 2009

Audit Area	Prior Year Actual	%	Current Year Budget	%	Current Year Actual	%	Var. from Budget	Explanation of Variance from Budget
Planning	6	2.6%						
Interim:								
Understanding internal control	5	2.1%						
Testing control design effectiveness	3	1.3%						
Testing control operting effectiveness	3	1.3%						
Cash	2	0.9%						
Accounts Receivable	2	0.9%						
Inventory	4	1.7%						
Fixed assets	2	0.9%						
Accounts Payable	2	0.9%						
Accrued liabilites	2	0.9%						
Federal income taxes	2	0.9%						
Notes Payable	2	0.9%						
Capital Stock	1	0.4%						
Retained Earnings	1	0.4%						
Operating accounts	2	0.9%						
Trial balance and adjusting entries	3	1.3%						
Other (Explain):								
Total Interim	36	15.4%						

45

Peach Blossom Cologne Company
Time Budget
December 31, 2009

Audit Area	Prior Year Actual	%	Current Year Budget	%	Current Year Actual	%	Var. from Budget	Explanation of Variance from Budget
Year-end:								
Cash	16	6.8%						
Accounts Receivable	18	7.7%						
Inventory	24	10.3%						
Fixed Assets	16	6.8%						
Accounts Payable	22	9.4%						
Accrued Liabilities	8	3.4%						
Federal Income Taxes	8	3.4%						
Notes Payable	7	3.0%						
Capital Stock	1	0.4%						
Retained Earnings	2	0.9%						
Operating accounts	14	6.0%						
Commitments & Contingencies	3	1.3%						
Minutes & Correspondence	6	2.6%						
Representations Letter	1	0.4%						
Unrecorded Liabilities	8	3.4%						
Report Preparation	8	3.4%						
Internal Control Letter	1	0.4%						
In-Charge Memorandum	5	2.1%						
Other (Explain):								
Total Year-end	168	71.8%						
Total Planning (from page 1)	6	2.6%						
Total Interim (from page 1)	36	15.4%						
Supervision & Review	24	10.3%						
Total Hours	234	100.0%						

PEACH BLOSSOM COLOGNE COMPANY

Organization Chart

PEACH BLOSSOM COLOGNE COMPANY

Flowchart of Financial Reporting Cycle
(Integration of Accounting Process)

Sales Order Entry and Accts Rec. (A/R & Sales)	Cash Receipts (Cash & A/R)	Accounts Payable (A/P & Inventory)	Cash Disbursements (Cash & A/P)	Bookkeeper	Controller	President, Other Managers (Monthly)

Assignment #2
Cash

The information that follows is grouped into two categories: 1) Internal Control and 2) Substantive Audit Procedures. This information is to be used to complete the exercises for this assignment.

Relevant Information

Internal Control

Peach Blossom Cologne Company's general disbursement checking account (account number 101) is with the Big City National Bank, Main at Michigan Avenue, Chicago, Illinois. It is used for all cash receipts and disbursements transactions.

The following internal control questionnaire pertaining to cash receipts, cash disbursements, and cash balances was completed by Jasper Parsons on December 15, 2009. Review this questionnaire carefully along with the Permanent File material describing the control environment, as well as the accounting and control procedures related to the various cash subsystems. Your firm has found that personnel involved in this area are generally competent.

As you read this material and analyze the internal control questionnaire, keep in mind the six control procedure categories: (1) segregation of duties, (2) access, (3) authorization, (4) input controls, (5) processing controls, and (6) output controls. Then consider possible errors or irregularities that could occur in the accounting system related to cash transactions and balances.

Typical errors or irregularities involving cash receipts, disbursements, and balances include:

Cash Receipts

1. Cash receipts may have been deposited in the bank but not recorded in the cash receipts journal.
2. Cash receipts may have been recorded but not deposited in the bank.
3. The offsetting credit for the cash receipt may have been placed in the wrong account.
4. The amount of cash receipts may have been incorrectly recorded.
5. Cash receipts may have been recorded in the wrong accounting period.

Cash Disbursements

1. Unauthorized disbursements may have occurred.
2. Disbursements may have been recorded but the check not mailed.
3. Disbursements may have been made but not recorded in the cash disbursements journal.
4. The disbursement may have been recorded in the wrong account.
5. Disbursements may have been recorded in the wrong accounting period.

Cash Balances

1. The bank reconciliation may have been purposefully misfooted to cover a defalcation.
2. The reconciliation may include fictitious deposits in transit.
3. Outstanding checks may have been omitted from the reconciliation to conceal a cash shortage.

Internal Control Questionnaire—Cash Transactions and Balances

Cash Receipts

Probably the most important control over cash receipts is the preparation of an independent record of those receipts for later reconciliation with the recorded accountability.

	Yes	No	Comments
1. Are all mail receipts recorded for control purposes?	√	–	
2. Does the person who opens the mail record the receipts immediately?	–	√	*Opened by G.Klett, the mail clerk, then routed to S.Swift, who prepares prelist.*
3. Are the mail receipts listed by a person who has no other cash or accounts receivable responsibilities?	–	√	*Prelisted by accounts receivable clerk.*
4. Is the list of mail receipts independently reconciled to the accounting records by a person who does not have access to cash receipts?	√	–	*By controller who initials reconciliation.*
5. Are bank deposits made by a person who does not prepare the deposit?	√	–	
6. Are the duties of the cashier separate from those of the accounts receivable clerk?	√	–	
7. Is a duplicate deposit ticket received by someone who does not prepare or make the deposit?	–	√	*Received by treasurer, who makes deposit and reconciles bank statement.*
8. Are receipts deposited intact daily?	√	–	

Cash Disbursements

	Yes	No	Comments
1. Are check signers independent of persons who approve cash disbursements?	–	√	*Controller signs checks and approves vouchers for payment.*
2. Are check signers independent of persons who post to the general ledger?	–	√	*Controller signs checks and also approves journal entries.*
3. Are check signers authorized by the board of directors?	√	–	
4. Are dual signatures utilized?	√	–	

50

	Yes	No	Comments
5. Are prenumbered checks used?	√	–	
6. Are voided checks properly mutilated and retained?	√	–	
7. Are all disbursements made by check except petty cash disbursements?	√	–	
8. Are blank checks properly controlled?	–	√	*The checks are left unlocked.*

Cash Balances

	Yes	No	Comments
1. Are bank accounts reconciled on a monthly basis?	√	–	
2. Are bank statements sent directly to the person who reconciles the bank account?	√	–	
3. Are bank accounts reconciled by a person who has no other cash responsibilities?	–	√	*Reconciled by treasurer.*

Substantive Audit Procedures: Cash Balances

Lillian Stockton, the treasurer, prepares the monthly bank reconciliation. Don McKenna provided you with a copy of the reconciliation for the month of December, 2009. You also obtained from Don selected portions of the cash receipts and cash disbursements journals. You have received directly from the bank the confirmation and cutoff bank statements that were requested January 4, 2010. The cutoff bank statements cover the period from January 1 to January 12, 2010.

The cutoff bank statement, along with items clearing during the cutoff period, which you requested from Big City National Bank, are shown in Exhibit 1. A selected portion of the cash receipts journal is provided as Exhibit 2, while a selected portion of the cash disbursements journal is shown in Exhibit 3. **You may assume that checks written in December and not shown as clearing on the cutoff bank statement cleared on the December bank statement.**

The following are the two working papers prepared for you by the client or obtained directly from the bank. The client prepared the bank reconciliation working paper, A-1. Having requested the bank confirmation from Big City National Bank, you received it (working paper A-2) directly from the bank.

	Reference
Bank reconciliation–Big City National Bank	A-1
Standard bank confirmation--Big City National Bank	A-2

Required Exercises

1. Prepare a substantive audit program to test cash balances. The construction of such a program should begin with the five financial statement assertions: (1) existence or occurrence, (2) completeness, (3) rights and obligations, (4) valuation or allocation, and (5) presentation and disclosure. You should derive your specific audit objectives for cash balances from these assertions. Your audit program should address the five financial statement assertions, as well as any internal control weaknesses you have uncovered. In this regard, keep in mind the six control procedure categories, as well as the other internal control elements. You may assume that you have satisfied yourself as to any assertions not specifically mentioned in the narrative.

    As you write your program, remember the generalized evidence-gathering procedures of (1) recalculation, (2) physical observation, (3) confirmation, (4) verbal inquiry, (5) vouching of documents, (6) tracing, (7) scanning, and (8) analytical procedures. Use them to help you write the specific evidence-gathering procedures in your program. Write your program on form AP-1. Use the financial statement assertions as the major headings, or captions, for your program.

2. Study the prior year's working papers, paying attention to the use of tick marks to indicate your audit procedures, and the system of cross-referencing among working papers.

    Gather evidence as necessary from the exhibits, the direct bank mailings, the client-prepared schedules, and your own observations to perform your audit work in the cash area by completing working papers A-1 and A-2.

    Important Note: Mr. Lancaster, President of Peach Blossom Cologne Company, has asked you to record every adjusting journal entry that you find, regardless of materiality. You should add any such adjustments to the applicable working paper and also record them on working paper AJE (Schedule of Adjusting Journal Entries) and the working trial balance (working paper TBBS-TBIS). Recording these adjustments on working papers AJE and TBBS-TBIS as you find them will reduce your workload at the end of the audit.

Substantive Audit Program–Cash Balances

Assertions

Begin with the list of assertions below and add others as you think appropriate. Then write your audit program to test those assertions.

1. The amount of cash is not materially more than the amount shown on the balance sheet.
2. All cash has been recorded.
3. Cash is correctly shown as a current asset.
4. Cash is not restricted to noncurrent use.

_____

_____

_____

_____

_____

_____

_____

_____

_____

_____

_____

_____

_____

_____

_____

_____

_____

_____

_____

_____

_____

_____

_____

Program Steps

EXHIBIT 1

BIG CITY NATIONAL BANK
Cutoff Bank Statement and Clearings

BIG CITY NATIONAL BANK					
Main at Michigan Avenue Chicago, Illinois 60612					
Statement of Account #58-4329					
			PEACH BLOSSOM COLOGNE COMPANY		

DATE	CHECKS			DEPOSITS	BALANCE
12-31-09	Balance forward				400,927
1-4-10	140	185		25,311	425,913
1-5-10	4,150			73,550	495,313
1-6-10	147,226			18,000	366,087
1-7-10	5,740	1,590		6,000	364,757
1-8-10	214	125	960	7,600	369,458
	1,600				
1-11-10	468	1,840	275	70,000	428,175
	8,700				
1-12-10	445	2,350			425,380

EXHIBIT 1 (Continued)

Deposit slips that agree with the above statement were received with the cutoff bank statement. The following is a list of paid checks that were received with the cutoff bank statement.

Check Number	Date of Check	Cleared Bank	Payee	Amount
1446	12-28	1-04	Longhorn Garbage Disposal	140
1449	12-29	1-04	DeBella Hardware	185
1445	12-28	1-05	Roberts and Underwood Insurance	4,150
1451	1-04	1-06	Fruit Juicy Perfume Co.	147,226
1452	1-04	1-07	Hammel, Hammel, & Johnson	5,740
1456	1-05	1-07	Barrows Office Supply	1,590
1465	1-06	1-08	Dr. Edward Abel	214
1444	12-28	1-08	Lawns by George	125
1450	12-29	1-08	Quick-Print Printers	960
1458	1-05	1-08	Apple Valley Security	1,600
1460	1-06	1-11	William F. Reimann	468
1459	1-05	1-11	Alex McBane	1,840
1464	1-06	1-11	Fulton Paper Co.	275
1455	1-04	1-11	Edwards, Overstreet, & Gilley	8,700
1454	1-04	1-12	Norton Exterminators	445
1461	1-06	1-12	Kalvin and Hubbs	2,350

EXHIBIT 2

CASH RECEIPTS JOURNAL
(selected portions)

| CASH DEBIT | DATE | SOURCE | CREDIT | |
			ACCOUNTS RECEIVABLE	OTHER
163,093	12-24-09	Total brought forward	163,093	0
25,800	12-28	Various A/R - Listed	25,800	
53,250	12-29	Various A/R - Listed	53,250	
25,311	12-31	Various A/R - Listed	25,311	
267,454	12-31-09	December totals	267,454	0
0	1-01-10	Beginning balance	0	0
73,550	1-05	Various A/R - Listed	73,550	
18,000	1-06	Young and Beautiful	18,000	
6,000	1-07	Incense, Inc.	6,000	
97,550	1-07-10	Totals forward to next page	97,550	0

EXHIBIT 3

CASH DISBURSEMENTS JOURNAL
(selected portions)

| | | Peach Blossom Cologne Company Cash Disbursements | | |
DATE	CHECK NUMBER	PAYEE	DEBIT ACCOUNT NUMBER	CASH CREDIT
12-26-09		Totals brought forward		212,000
12-28	1444	Lawns by George	301	125
12-28	1445	Roberts and Underwood Ins.	301	4,150
12-28	1446	Longhorn Garbage Disp.	301	140
12-28	1447	Gulf States Oil Supply	830	80
12-28	1448	United Fund	832	25
12-29	1449	DeBella Hardware	301	185
12-29	1450	Quick-Print Printers	301	960
12-31-09		December totals		217,665
1-04-10	1451	Fruit Juicy Perfume Co.	301	147,226
1-04	1452	Hammel, Hammel, & Johnson	301	5,740
1-04	1453	Mid-Town Office Supply	112	3,800
1-04	1454	Norton Exterminators	301	445
1-04	1455	Edwards, Overstreet, and Gilley	301	8,700
1-05	1456	Barrows Office Supply	301	1,590
1-05	1457	Central Power and Light	301	1,400
1-05	1458	Apple Valley Security	832	1,600
1-05	1459	Alex McBane	301	1,840
1-06	1460	William F. Reimann	301	468
1-06	1461	Kalvin and Hubbs	301	2,350
1-06	1462	Fruit Juicy Perfume Co	301	8,064
1-06	1463	Hoffmann Supply Co.	301	240
1-06	1464	Fulton Paper Co.	301	275
1-06	1465	Dr. Edward Abel	832	214
1-07	1466	Flash Freight Co.	301	340
1-07-10		Totals carried forward		184,292

	Peach Blossom Cologne Company					A-1		
	Bank Reconciliation - Big City National Bank							
	December 31, 2009							
	(Prepared by Client)							
	Balance Per Bank Statement				400927			
	Add:							
	Deposit in transit		Dec 31		25311			
	Deduct: Checks outstanding							
No.	Payee							
1444	Lawns by George		Dec. 28	125				
1445	Roberts & Underwood Ins.		Dec. 28	4150				
1446	Longhorn Garbage Disposal		Dec. 28	140				
1449	DeBella Hardware		Dec. 29	185				
1450	Quick Print Printers		Dec. 29	960	5560			
	Balance 12-31-09				420678			

STANDARD FORM TO CONFIRM ACCOUNT
BALANCE INFORMATION WITH FINANCIAL INSTITUTIONS

ORIGINAL
To be mailed to accountant

Peach Blossom Cologne Co.

CUSTOMER NAME

We have provided to our accountants the following information as of the close of business on **December 31, XX 2009** regarding our deposit and loan balances. Please confirm the accuracy of the information, noting any exceptions to the information provided. If the balances have been left blank, please complete this form by furnishing the balances in the appropriate spaces below.* Although we do not request nor expect you to conduct a comprehensive, detailed search of your records, if during the process of completing this confirmation additional information about other deposit and loan accounts we may have with you comes to your attention, please include such information below. Please use the enclosed envelope to return the form directly to our accountants.

Financial Institution's Name and Address

[Big City National Bank
Big City National Bank Building
Main at Michigan Avenue
{ Chicago, Illinois 60612]

1. At the close of business on the date listed above, our records indicated the following deposit balance(s):

ACCOUNT NAME	ACCOUNT NO.	INTEREST RATE	BALANCE*
Peach Blossom Cologne Company	58-4329	N/A	$400,927

2. We were directly liable to the financial institution for loans at the close of business on the date listed above as follows:

ACCOUNT NO./ DESCRIPTION	BALANCE*	DATE DUE	INTEREST RATE	DATE THROUGH WHICH INTEREST IS PAID	DESCRIPTION OF COLLATERAL

Lillian Stockton
(Customer's Authorized Signature)

January 4, 2010
(Date)

The information presented above by the customer is in agreement with our records. Although we have not conducted a comprehensive, detailed search of our records, no other deposit or loan accounts have come to our attention except as noted below.

Rudol Churchill
(Financial Institution Authorized Signature)

January 8, 2010
(Date)

Cashier
(Title)

EXCEPTIONS AND/OR COMMENTS

Please return this form directly to our accountants:

[Anderson, Olds, and Watershed
615 Big City National Bank Bldg.
Main at Michigan Avenue
Chicago, Illinois 60612
[ ]

* Ordinarily, balances are intentionally left blank if they are not available at the time the form is prepared.

Approved 1990 by American Bankers Association, American Institute of Certified Public Accountants, and Bank Administration Institute. Additional forms available from: AICPA – Order Department, P.O. Box 1003, NY, NY 10108-1003

D 451 5951

Assignment #3
Accounts Receivable and Credit Sales

The information that follows is grouped into two categories: (1) Internal Control and (2) Substantive Audit Procedures. This information is to be used to complete the exercises for this assignment. *Do the optional exercises only if told to do so by your instructor.*

Relevant Information

Internal Control

The following internal control questionnaire was completed by Jasper Parsons. Review this questionnaire carefully. Also, read the permanent file material describing the control environment and the accounting procedures related to the Credit Sales System. As you read this material and go through the questionnaire, keep in mind the six categories of control procedures: (1) segregation of functions, (2) access, (3) authorization, (4) input controls, (5) processing controls and (6) output controls. Then try to determine the possible errors or irregularities that could occur.

Typical errors or irregularities include:

1. Sales amounts may have been incorrectly recorded
2. Goods may have been shipped but not billed to the customer
3. Sales may have been billed to the customer but not shipped
4. Sales may have been recorded in the wrong accounting period
5. Merchandise may have been sold to customers who were bad credit risks
6. Unauthorized sales may have occurred
7. Sales may have been posted to the wrong account
8. Unauthorized write-offs of receivables may have occurred.

Internal Control Questionnaire—Credit Sales system

	Yes	No	Comments
1. Are customer subsidiary ledgers maintained by a person who has no access to cash?	_	√	*Accounts receivable clerk has access to customer checks and cash prelist.*
2. Are unauthorized persons unable to obtain access to customer accounts?	_	√	*All LAN reports and printouts are left unlocked and are accessible to anyone. Additionally, the cashier has access to the LAN accounts receivable application.*
3. Is a record maintained of accounts previously written off?	√	_	

4. Are credit sales approved by the credit manager before shipment? √ _ _____

5. Are sales orders approved by the sales manager? √ _ _____

6. Are write-offs of bad debts approved by an official not associated with the selling or credit functions? _ √ *Approved by Brenda Robertson, who initials them.*

7. Are credit memos approved by a responsible official? √ _ *Approved by Ellen Jacobs, who initials them.*

8. Are invoices prenumbered and controlled? √ _ _____

9. Are sales invoices checked as to prices and mechanical accuracy? _ √ *Client considers it not cost effective.*

10. Are credit memos prenumbered and controlled? √ _ _____

11. Are numbered shipping documents prepared for all shipments? √ _ _____

12. Are accounts aged periodically? √ _ *Monthly.*

13. Are customer subsidiary ledgers reconciled with the control account periodically? √ _ *Balancing report is produced by LAN software.*

14. Are customers billed by someone who has no other sales or accounts receivable responsibilities? _ √ *Billed by the bookkeeper, Don McKenna, who records journal entries*

Substantive Audit Procedures: Accounts Receivable and Bad Debts

To begin your substantive audit work in the accounts receivable area, you obtained an aged trial balance from Don McKenna. This schedule is included in the working papers with this assignment section referenced B-1. You may assume that you can check the aged trial balance with the accounts receivable subsidiary ledger and that the subsidiary ledger supports the aged trial balance as to both amounts due and age of accounts.

On Monday, January 4, with the client's assistance, you prepared and mailed both positive and negative accounts receivable confirmations. Positive confirmations were sent to the following five customers with balances over $7,500: (1) Anne Charlotte Cosmetics, (2) Darings, (3) Frankie's Floral Fragrances, (4) Tears and Doefall Company, (5) Young and Beautiful. Negative confirmations were mailed to all other customers with an accounts receivable balance. None of the confirmations was returned by the Post Office because of inability to deliver. You have received replies on all of the positive confirmations and no replies to the negative confirmations. The positive confirmations are referenced B-2 through B-4.

You have also discussed the accounts with Brenda Robertson, and she had the following comments about the delinquent accounts and their paying habits:

Customer	Paying Habits
Alpha Aroma	Good account.
Anne Charlotte Cosmetics	Good account.
Bobell Beauty Supply	Never been delinquent before.
Body Bar	Slow paying, good account.
Capitol Odors	Probably will collect nothing.
Cut-Rate Discount Stores	Slow paying, but has always paid.
Darings	Established company, good pay.
Incense, Inc.	Never been delinquent before.
Janis Dept. Store	Slow paying, good account.
Rausch's Department Store	Sometimes slow, good account.

Brenda Robertson indicated that she had spoken with both Parker Shelton, controller, and Ellen Jacobs, sales manager, about the delinquent Capital Odors account. They were in agreement that it should be written off. Accounts amounting to $14,335 had been written off during the year; you noted that all write-offs were approved by Ms. Robertson.

From the January cash receipts journal you were able to learn of the following subsequent payments on the accounts receivables balances as of December 31, 2009.

Customer	Payment Amount	Payment Date
Alpha Aroma	$2,050	1-14
Anne Charlotte Cosmetics	32,350	1-04
Body Bar	1,850	1-08
Cut-Rate Discount Stores	1,800	1-08
Darings	36,000	1-04
Incense, Inc.	6,000	1-07
Janis Department Store	5,200	1-04
Lone Star Supply	3,290	1-14
Rausch's Department Store	3,950	1-08
Tears and Doefall Company	70,000	1-11
Young and Beautiful	18,000	1-06
Total	$180,490	

Exercises

Part A–Audit of Internal Control (Optional)

1. Using the narrative in the permanent file, as well as the information from the internal control questionnaire above, prepare a business process flowchart on form P-4 for the Credit Sales System, or using software, label the form P-4. The headings have been set out for you on form P-4. Show the flow of documentation, the steps involved in the process and note any internal control features.

2. Using the flowchart, the internal control questionnaire, and the system narrative, describe the control procedures (strengths) in the system of controls over Credit Sales. For each control procedure, describe a test of control you could perform to test the operating effectiveness of the control. Use form CSF-1. Keep in mind the six categories of control procedures: (1) segregation of duties, (2) access limited to authorized persons, (3) authorization for the proper execution of transactions, (4) input controls, (5) processing controls, and (6) output controls. Classify the strengths under these six captions.

3. For each weakness you find in the controls related to credit sales, list the weakness, a possible error or irregularity that could occur because of the weakness, and a compensating substantive test of transactions or balances to detect the error or irregularity assuming the necessary records and documents are available to you. Use form CWF-1. Classify the weaknesses under the six categories of control procedures as outlined in (2) above. You should keep these weaknesses in mind, as well as the five financial statement assertions when you write the substantive audit steps for your programs to audit the financial statements.

4. ALTERNATIVE A–Tests of Controls
   Prepare an audit program consisting of tests of controls to test whether the company's internal control procedures related to credit sales are operating effectively. Utilize the analysis of strengths you have prepared to guide you, remembering to keep the internal control objectives and financial statement assertions in mind. Write your test of controls audit program on form SP-1.

   ALTERNATIVE B–Tests of Controls and Substantive Tests of Transactions

   Prepare an audit program to test the business processes related to credit sales. Your program should consist of: (1) tests of controls to test the control procedures; (2) substantive tests of details of transactions; and/or (3) dual-purpose tests having both test of control and substantive aspects. Utilize the analysis of strengths and weaknesses you have prepared to guide you, remembering to keep internal control objectives and the financial statement assertions in mind. Write your system audit program on form SP-1. Use the headings: *Tests of Controls, Dual-Purpose Tests, and Substantive Tests of Transactions*. List the appropriate audit steps under each of these headings.

   Note: When analyzing internal control by working the optional exercises in this assignment, identify the audit program step that addresses the strength or weakness in internal control by cross-referencing the program step to each strength with an "S" and each weakness with a "W" (e.g., S-1, S-2, W-1, W-2, etc.).

PART B–Attributes Sampling Exercise (Optional)

You have decided to conduct a test of controls using attributes sampling methods to determine the extent to which sales invoices are supported by a shipping document. There should be a shipping document for each sales invoice. During the year, Peach Blossom issued 468 sales invoices, numbered 20099 to 20566.

You have decided that for purposes of this test that the tolerable deviation rate should be 4% with an expected population deviation rate of 0% and an acceptable risk of assessing control risk too low of .05 (the risk of assessing control risk too low is also known as *the acceptable risk of overreliance* or ARO). Use the tables provided with the materials at the end of this assignment to determine the sample size. According to the Anderson, Olds, and Watershed audit manual, a small population such as this one should be reduced using the following finite correction factor:

$$n = \frac{n'}{1 + n'/N}$$

where   n'   = sample size obtained from the table
       N   = population size
       n   = corrected sample size.

Required:
1. State the objective of the test.
2. Specify the attribute and the exception condition.
3. Define the population and the sampling unit.
4. Determine the appropriate sample size after applying the finite correction factor.
5. Select the invoices to be included in your sample. Use a random number table or spreadsheet software to generate random numbers (e.g., in EXCEL, use Random Number Generation under Tools, Data Analysis) for this purpose.
6. Assume that you examine each invoice selected. During 2009, Peach Blossom issued 468 sales invoices, numbered 20099 to 20566. Regarding shipping documents, this population of sales invoices has the following characteristics: 437 invoices are supported by shipping documents. The following thirty-one invoices are not supported by a shipping document:

20100	20178	20310	20364	20487	20552
20112	20209	20321	20381	20497	
20121	20232	20324	20391	20510	
20143	20240	20329	20399	20522	
20149	20261	20333	20412	20439	
20155	20298	20357	20418	20542	

(Of course the auditor would not have information regarding the errors in the population. However, use this information to identify those invoices in your sample having a deviation.)
7. Based on the number of deviations you have found in your sample, state the sample error rate and the achieved upper error rate using the evaluation table provided in this assignment.
8. State your conclusion. If you conclude that controls are not operating effectively, state the compensating substantive test(s) that you would perform.

Use the attributes sampling tables included with the material at the end of this assignment to determine the sample size and evaluate results. Consult your textbook for information on attributes sampling. Guidance is also provided in the AICPA Audit Guide, *Audit Sampling*, pp. 15-29 (AICPA 2001).

PART C–Required Exercises: Substantive Procedures

1. Prepare a substantive audit program to test accounts receivable balances and bad debts. The construction of such a program should begin with an explicit recognition of the five financial statement assertions: (1) existence or occurrence, (2) completeness, (3) rights and obligations, (4) valuation or allocation, and (5) presentation and disclosure. You should derive your specific audit objectives for accounts receivable and bad debts from these assertions. Your audit program should address the five financial statement assertions, as well as any internal control weaknesses that you

have uncovered. In this regard, keep in mind the six categories of control procedures, as well as the other internal control elements. You may assume that you have satisfied yourself as to any assertions not specifically mentioned in the narrative.

As you write your program, remember the generalized evidence-gathering procedures of (1) recalculation, (2) physical observation, (3) confirmation, (4) verbal inquiry, (5) vouching of documents, (6) tracing, (7) scanning, and (8) analytical procedures. Use them to help you write the specific evidence-gathering procedures in your program. Write your audit program on form AP-2. Use the financial statement assertions as the major headings or captions for your program. List the appropriate steps under each of these headings.

> Note: As you go through the audit, whenever you prepare an audit program to test the substantive details of balances, identify the program step that addresses the weakness in internal control by referencing the appropriate question from the internal control questionnaire (e.g., Q-1, Q-2, etc.). If you have conducted a formal analysis of internal control by having worked the optional exercises, then you should cross-reference your program steps to the relevant weaknesses you have identified (W-1, W-2, and so on).

2. Study the prior year working papers, schedules B-1 through B-5. Note the use of "tick marks" to evidence the audit work and the system of cross-referencing the working papers. Perform all required audit work on the current year's schedules B-1 through B-4 and prepare schedule B-5 to analyze the allowance account for the current year, performing all appropriate audit work. You have determined that the expected uncollectible percentages from the prior year are still appropriate for the current year.

PEACH BLOSSOM COLOGNE COMPANY

Credit Sales

Sales

Credit Manager

Stores (Warehouse/Repack)

Shipping

Bookkeeper

Accounts Receivable Clerk

Credit Sales
Internal Control Strengths

Strength	Possible Test of Controls

Credit Sales
Internal Control Weaknesses

Weakness	Potential Error	Compensating Substantive Procedure

Credit Sales
Program

STATISTICAL SAMPLING TABLES

Statistical Sample Sizes for Test of Controls—5 Percent Risk of Assessing Control Risk Too Low
(with number of expected errors in parentheses)

Expected Population Deviation Rate	Tolerable Rate										
	2%	3%	4%	5%	6%	7%	8%	9%	10%	15%	20%
0.00%	149(0)	99(0)	74(0)	59(0)	49(0)	42(0)	36(0)	32(0)	29(0)	19(0)	14(0)
.25	236(1)	157(1)	117(1)	93(1)	78(1)	66(1)	58(1)	51(1)	46(1)	30(1)	22(1)
.50	*	157(1)	117(1)	93(1)	78(1)	66(1)	58(1)	51(1)	46(1)	30(1)	22(1)
.75	*	208(2)	117(1)	93(1)	78(1)	66(1)	58(1)	51(1)	46(1)	30(1)	22(1)
1.00	*	*	156(2)	93(1)	78(1)	66(1)	58(1)	51(1)	46(1)	30(1)	22(1)
1.25	*	*	156(2)	124(2)	78(1)	66(1)	58(1)	51(1)	46(1)	30(1)	22(1)
1.50	*	*	192(3)	124(2)	103(2)	66(1)	58(1)	51(1)	46(1)	30(1)	22(1)
1.75	*	*	227(4)	153(3)	103(2)	88(2)	77(2)	51(1)	46(1)	30(1)	22(1)
2.00	*	*	*	181(4)	127(3)	88(2)	77(2)	68(2)	46(1)	30(1)	22(1)
2.25	*	*	*	208(5)	127(3)	88(2)	77(2)	68(2)	61(2)	30(1)	22(1)
2.50	*	*	*	*	150(4)	109(3)	77(2)	68(2)	61(2)	30(1)	22(1)
2.75	*	*	*	*	173(5)	109(3)	95(3)	68(2)	61(2)	30(1)	22(1)
3.00	*	*	*	*	195(6)	129(4)	95(3)	84(3)	61(2)	30(1)	22(1)
3.25	*	*	*	*	*	148(5)	112(4)	84(3)	61(2)	30(1)	22(1)
3.50	*	*	*	*	*	167(6)	112(4)	84(3)	76(3)	40(2)	22(1)
3.75	*	*	*	*	*	185(7)	129(5)	100(4)	76(3)	40(2)	22(1)
4.00	*	*	*	*	*	*	146(6)	100(4)	89(4)	40(2)	22(1)
5.00	*	*	*	*	*	*	*	158(8)	116(6)	40(2)	30(2)
6.00	*	*	*	*	*	*	*	*	179(11)	50(3)	30(2)
7.00	*	*	*	*	*	*	*	*	*	68(5)	37(3)

* Sample size is too large to be cost-effective for most audit applications.
Note: This table assumes a large population. For discussion of the effect of population size on sample size, see chapter 3.

Statistical Sampling Results Evaluation Table for Tests of Controls—Upper Limits at 5 Percent Risk of Assessing Control Risk Too Low

Sample Size	Actual Number of Deviations Found										
	0	1	2	3	4	5	6	7	8	9	10
25	11.3	17.6	*	*	*	*	*	*	*	*	*
30	9.5	14.9	19.6	*	*	*	*	*	*	*	*
35	8.3	12.9	17.0	*	*	*	*	*	*	*	*
40	7.3	11.4	15.0	18.3	*	*	*	*	*	*	*
45	6.5	10.2	13.4	16.4	19.2	*	*	*	*	*	*
50	5.9	9.2	12.1	14.8	17.4	19.9	*	*	*	*	*
55	5.4	8.4	11.1	13.5	15.9	18.2	*	*	*	*	*
60	4.9	7.7	10.2	12.5	14.7	16.8	18.8	*	*	*	*
65	4.6	7.1	9.4	11.5	13.6	15.5	17.4	19.3	*	*	*
70	4.2	6.6	8.8	10.8	12.6	14.5	16.3	18.0	19.7	*	*
75	4.0	6.2	8.2	10.1	11.8	13.6	15.2	16.9	18.5	20.0	*
80	3.7	5.8	7.7	9.5	11.1	12.7	14.3	15.9	17.4	18.9	*
90	3.3	5.2	6.9	8.4	9.9	11.4	12.8	14.2	15.5	16.8	18.2
100	3.0	4.7	6.2	7.6	9.0	10.3	11.5	12.8	14.0	15.2	16.4
125	2.4	3.8	5.0	6.1	7.2	8.3	9.3	10.3	11.3	12.3	13.2
150	2.0	3.2	4.2	5.1	6.0	6.9	7.8	8.6	9.5	10.3	11.1
200	1.5	2.4	3.2	3.9	4.6	5.2	5.9	6.5	7.2	7.8	8.4

* Over 20 percent
Note: This table presents upper limits as percentages. This table assumes a large population.

Substantive Audit Program–Accounts Receivable and Bad Debts

Assertions

Begin with the list of assertions below and add others you think appropriate. Then write your audit program to test those assertions.

1. None of the accounts receivable are fictitious.
2. No accounts receivable have been omitted from the balance sheet.
3. The accounts receivable are collectible in the normal course of business.
4. The accounts receivable are bona fide claims owed the company.
5. Pledged accounts receivable or accounts receivable used as collateral are disclosed.
6. Receivables from directors, officers, and affiliates are separately disclosed.

Program Steps

_____

_____

_____

_____

_____

_____

_____

_____

_____

_____

_____

_____

_____

_____

_____

_____

_____

_____

_____

_____

Peach Blossom Cologne Company

B-1

Accounts Receivable - Aged Trial Balance

12-31-09

(Prepared by Client)

Customer	Current 1-30 days	30-60 Days	60-90 Days	Over 90 Days	Total	Confirmation Mailed	Subsequent Collection	Comments by Credit Manager--
Alpha Aroma	1150	900			2050			
Anne Charlotte Cosmetics	30900	1450			32350			
Bobell Beauty Supplies		1460			1460			
Body Bar	2100	800	1050		3950			
Capitol Odors				1200	1200			
Cut-Rate Discount Stores	2380	1720	400		4500			
Darings	35500	7600			43100			
Frankies Floral Frag.	20400				20400			
Incense, Inc.	6300	600			6900			
Janis Department Stores		4600	1150		5750			
Lone Star Supply	3290				3290			
Rausch's Dept.Store	2700	1250			3950			
Tears and Doefall Co.	75450				75450			
William's Fragrances	1850				1850			
Young and Beautiful	24350				24350			
Various Other Acct's.	4830				4830			
Per client	211200	20380	2600	1200	235380			

74

Assignment #4
Inventory and Purchases

The information that follows is grouped into two categories: (1) Internal Control and (2) Substantive Audit Procedures. This information is to be used to complete the exercises for this assignment. *Do the optional exercises only if told to do so by your instructor.*

Relevant Information

Internal Control

The Peach Blossom Cologne Company charges the net cost (including related freight, taxes, and discounts) of inventory purchases directly to the Inventory account. The company keeps a perpetual inventory record. At each year-end, a physical inventory is taken in order to adjust the Cost of Goods Sold account to the physical count. Any differences between the physical count and the perpetual records are charged or credited to Cost of Goods Sold.

Peach Blossom purchases the bulk of its inventory from two sources: Fruit Scents, Inc., in Hope, Michigan, and Fruit Juicy Perfume Company in Springfield, Missouri. All inventory is purchased by the case with each case holding 24 units (bottles, jars, or cans). All inventory received from vendors is stored in the warehouse until needed.

A voucher system is used for purchases. Vouchers are prepared when invoices are received and held in an unpaid voucher file (filed by payment date) until the cash disbursement is made. A voucher number is a two-number code with the first number representing the month in which the voucher was recorded and the second number representing the order in which the voucher was recorded during the month. For example, 10-7 would be the number for the seventh invoice recorded during the month of October.

Peach Blossom Cologne Company is a wholesale distributor. Products received from factory vendors are repackaged and distributed to retailers. Orders are processed as received from customers. As soon as an order is completed, it is shipped immediately. Timeliness is important because the company has very little room to store repackaged merchandise.

The following internal control questionnaire was completed for you by Jasper Parsons. Review this questionnaire and the permanent file material describing the control procedures related to Inventory-Purchases. Your firm has found that personnel involved in this area are generally competent.

The Inventory-Purchases system initiates a business process that begins with the requisition and purchase of materials and then proceeds to the recording of the liability for the purchase. You will study the recording of the liability for purchases in Assignment #6, which deals with accounts payable processing. As you read through the inventory and purchases material and analyze the questionnaire, keep in mind the six categories of control procedures: (1) segregation of duties, (2) access, (3) authorization, (4) input controls, (5) processing controls, and (6) output controls, as well as potential errors or irregularities.

Typical errors or irregularities in the inventory and purchases area include:

1. Inventory may have been shipped but not recorded.

2. Inventory usage may not have been accurately recorded.
3. Purchases may have been recorded but the merchandise not received.
4. Merchandise may have been received but not recorded in purchases.
5. Purchases may have been recorded erroneously.
6. Unauthorized purchases may have been made.
7. Inventory may have been stolen.
8. Inventory may have been improperly counted.
9. Inventory may have been improperly valued.

Internal Control Questionnaire–Inventory-Purchases System

		Yes	No	Comments
1.	Is a physical inventory taken at least annually?	√	—	
2.	Does the company prepare written instructions for inventory counts?	√	—	
3.	Are such instructions followed by those taking the physical count?	√	—	
4.	Are the inventory counts taken by personnel who are independent of the custody or recording of inventory?	—	√	*Anita Columbo, the inventory clerk, helps count inventory.*
5.	Are the inventories adequately safeguarded and controlled?	√	—	
6.	Is a receiving report prepared for all receipts of merchandise?	√	—	
7.	Is the purchasing function independent of receiving and accounting?	—	√	*Receiving and purchasing are in the same department.*
8.	Are purchase requisitions used?	√	—	
9.	Are prenumbered purchase orders used?	√	—	
10.	Are purchases authorized by responsible officials?	√	—	*Mr. Brown signs the purchase orders.*
11.	Are all receipts properly counted and inspected?	√	—	
12.	Does the company maintain a perpetual inventory system?	√	—	

13. Are such records maintained by someone who does not have custody of inventory? __ √

Anita Columbo also maintains the inventory master records.

14. Are discrepancies between the physical count and the perpetual records investigated periodically? √ __

The controller maintains tight control over inventory discrepancies.

Substantive Audit Procedures–Inventory Balances

On January 1, when the client took the physical inventory, you were on hand to observe the count. Since the plant was shut down for the inventory taking on January 1, 2010, all finished goods were shipped prior to the shutdown. You may assume that there are no shipping cut-off problems. To facilitate the counting of inventory in the warehouse, the client moved some of it out onto the shipping dock. Both inventory areas were neat and orderly. You satisfied yourself that the client was using good control procedures. During your conversations with various client personnel you also formed the opinion that the inventory personnel were reasonably competent. When the inventory was completed, you obtained all count sheets from the client and summarized them on a working paper. This was done in order to allow you to agree the total count with the final priced inventory. This work sheet summarizing all the count sheets is presented as schedule C-2. As you observed the inventory, you recorded several test counts. These test counts are noted on schedule C-2 by a tick mark (n). You should prepare an inventory observation memorandum describing the work you did and any problems encountered or observed during the entire inventory count procedure. (A form for that memorandum is referenced C-3.)

Don McKenna has compiled the final inventory, pricing it on a FIFO basis. He has provided you with a copy of that inventory, and it is presented in the working papers as schedule C-1. You may assume that you have checked current replacement costs on all the inventory items and found that each exceeds its inventory carrying value.

You also asked Don McKenna to pull from the files the cash vouchers (along with supporting materials) for all inventory recorded as purchases by the Company for the current year. He did so and all the information from those vouchers has been summarized for you in Exhibit 4. (Exhibit 4 is being presented to you in lieu of the actual documents; as such, consider the material to represent the actual client documents belonging to the client and not the auditor.) You may assume that all vouchers have the appropriate supporting materials attached, that all vouchers have been properly approved, and that all information on the vendor's invoices is accurate. Use this information to perform the appropriate audit procedures.

Exercises

Part A–Assessing Audit Risk (Optional Exercises)

Before working the risk assessment exercises that follow, review the section entitled, *Assessing Audit Risk*, in the *General Instructions and Preparations* section of the case. To use the audit risk model for estimating the nature, extent, and timing of evidence, the auditor must first establish an acceptable overall audit risk (AR), then assess inherent risk (IR) and control risk (CR) for each assertion. The five financial statement assertions are (1) existence or occurrence, (2) completeness, (3) rights and obligations, (4) valuation or allocation, and (5) presentation and disclosure. Inherent risk is the probability that a misstatement occurs in an assertion. The more complex or subjective the account or class of transactions, the greater the inherent risk. The auditor assesses inherent risk by evaluating complexity, subjectivity, and related factors that may impact the risk of misstatements occurring in the account or class of transactions. The auditor assesses control risk by evaluating the effectiveness of controls in preventing or detecting material misstatements related to the assertion. After obtaining an understanding of internal control, the auditor determines an "assessed level of control risk." For a particular assertion, the assessed level may be 1.0 (100%), meaning the controls related to that assertion are nonexistent or not effective. If the auditor identifies controls that appear to be effective in preventing or detecting misstatements, the auditor may assess control risk at a level less than 1.0. If the assessed level is less than 1.0, the auditor has to support this assessment by performing tests of controls to determine whether the controls are effectively designed and are operating properly.

1. You have decided to assess the *inherent risk* associated with the assertion regarding the existence of inventory, specifically the assertion that "inventories included in the balance sheet physically exist." The Anderson, Olds, and Watershed audit manual sets out inherent risk assessments for various accounts and classes of transactions that you are able to use as a guide for setting inherent risk. The risk assessments in the audit manual use the following qualitative levels: *low, moderate, high*, and *maximum*. A low assessment corresponds to a .25 probability, moderate to .50, high to .75 and maximum to 1.0. The audit manual states that inherent risk associated with inventory assertions should normally not be designated at less than a "moderate" level. Write a memorandum for the file indicating what characteristics of inventory would indicate that an assessment of inherent risk at less than moderate is usually not warranted. Also state your assessment of inherent risk for the *existence* assertion.

2. Examine the internal control questionnaire for Inventory-Purchases. Identify those controls that directly relate to the assertion, "inventories in the balance sheet physically exist." For each control identified, describe a misstatement that could occur if the control is not effective.

3. Assess the *control risk* with regard to the assertion, "inventories included in the balance sheet physically exist." That is, assess how likely it would be that a material misstatement was not prevented or detected by the controls present in the Peach Blossom Cologne Company. Assess the control risk as either *low, moderate, high,* or *maximum*.

4. Anderson, Olds, and Watershed would like to keep the overall audit risk (AR) at .03. Based on the inherent risk assessment in Exercise (1) above, your control risk assessment in Exercise (3) above, and an overall audit risk (AR) of .03, compute the *acceptable detection risk*. Associate the probabilities outlined in Exercise (1) with the qualitative risk levels you selected for inherent risk and control risk. On the basis of your calculation of detection risk, describe in a memorandum the timing and extent of your substantive testing related to the existence of inventory. In your memorandum, explain the specific substantive audit tests you would conduct to verify existence. For each test, specify the timing of the test (interim or year-end) and designate the extent of testing. Use the following designations for the extent of testing: *minimum, moderate, extensive*. Explain why you chose that level of testing.

PART B–Dollar-Unit (PPS) Variables Sampling (Optional Exercise)

You have decided to conduct a substantive test to determine whether recorded purchases are overstated. You will use dollar-unit (PPS) sampling for this test. The purchase vouchers that have been recorded by the client during the year are listed in Exhibit 4. The total of these vouchers is $1,474,795 (including the vouchers for freight). You have decided that for purposes of this test, your tolerable misstatement should be $70,000. You expect a misstatement in the population of $15,000 based on experience with similar clients. The Anderson, Olds, and Watershed audit manual states that the acceptable risk of incorrect acceptance (ARIA) should be set at .05.

You will be selecting your sample from the population of the 1,474,795 dollars comprising purchases. The logical units that the dollars "hook" into are the thirteen vouchers listed in Exhibit 4. The sample size is calculated as follows:

$$\text{Sample size} = \frac{\text{Population book value} \times \text{Reliability factor}}{\text{Tolerable misstatement} - (\text{Expected misstatement} \times \text{Expansion factor})}$$

Required:
1. State the objective of the test.
2. Define the population and the sampling unit.
3. Determine the appropriate sample size using the formula given above and the tables provided at the end of this assignment (round *up* to the nearest whole number). Calculate the sampling interval. Assume that misstated items are in error by the full dollar amount of the recorded value (100% misstatement).
4. Select the dollars to be included in your sample and determine the logical units (vouchers) to be selected for audit using systematic selection. (Be sure to use the total amount for each voucher as indicated by the double underlining. Also be sure to include the vouchers for freight.) Use a random start of 13,732. Spreadsheet software facilitates the calculations.
5. Assume that you perform auditing procedures (consisting of the examination of documents supporting the vouchers) on the vouchers associated with the dollars selected. The following information about the errors in the population of vouchers would not be known by the auditor. Nevertheless, you should use this information to determine which of the vouchers in your sample contain errors:

   For purposes of this exercise only, assume that the logical units (vouchers) in the population contain the following errors:

Voucher No.	Recorded Amount	Correct Amount
6-27	$202,245	$182,245
12-38	8,487	4,887

   None of the other ten vouchers contains an error. (Note: *do not* prepare an adjustment for working paper TBBS-TBIS for errors discovered.)

6. Evaluate the results by determining the error bound for overstatements.
7. State your conclusion regarding the recorded balance of purchases. Use the Dollar Unit Sampling tables in this assignment to calculate the upper error bound. What action would you suggest the auditors should take at this point?

   (Note: to determine the upper error bound, consult the AICPA Audit Guide, *Audit Sampling,* pp. 55-69, AICPA, 2001).

PART C—Required Exercises: Substantive Procedures

1. Prepare a substantive audit program for inventory balances. The construction of an audit program for inventory balances should begin with an explicit recognition of the five financial statement assertions. As you write your program, keep these assertions in mind: (1) existence or occurrence, (2) completeness, (3) rights and obligations, (4) valuation or allocation, and (5) presentation and disclosure. From these assertions, you should derive your specific audit objectives related to inventory balances.

    Your audit program should address the five financial statement assertions, as well as any internal control weaknesses you have discovered. In this regard, keep in mind the six categories of internal control. You may assume that you have satisfied yourself with respect to any assertions not specifically mentioned in the narrative.

    As you write your program, remember the generalized evidence-gathering procedures of (1) recalculation, (2) physical observation, (3) confirmation, (4) verbal inquiry, (5) vouching of documents, (6) tracing, (7) scanning, and (8) analytical procedures. Use them to help you write the specific evidence-gathering procedures in your program.

    Write your program on form AP-3. Use the financial statement assertions as your major headings.

2. Study the prior year's working papers C-1 to C-3. Then perform all required audit work on schedules C-1 and C-2 and write your inventory observation memorandum; reference the memorandum C-3. Inventory adjustments that affect accounts payable are deferred until Assignment #6. Adjustments found in inventory that affect both inventory and accounts payable should be included on both the inventory and accounts payable working papers.

DOLLAR UNIT SAMPLING TABLES

Reliability Factors for Misstatements of Overstatement

Number of Overstatement Misstatements	Risk of Incorrect Acceptance								
	1%	*5%*	*10%*	*15%*	*20%*	*25%*	*30%*	*37%*	*50%*
0	4.61	3.00	2.31	1.90	1.61	1.39	1.21	1.00	.70
1	*6.64*	*4.75*	3.89	3.38	3.00	2.70	2.44	2.14	1.68
2	8.41	6.30	*5.33*	4.72	4.28	3.93	3.62	*3.25*	2.68
3	10.05	*7.76*	*6.69*	6.02	*5.52*	5.11	4.77	4.34	3.68
4	11.61	9.16	8.00	7.27	6.73	6.28	*5.90*	*5.43*	4.68
5	13.11	10.52	9.28	8.50	7.91	7.43	7.01	6.49	*5.68*
6	14.57	11.85	10.54	9.71	9.08	*8.56*	8.12	*7.56*	*6.67*
7	16.00	13.15	11.78	10.90	10.24	9.69	9.21	8.63	7.67
8	17.41	14.44	13.00	12.08	11.38	10.81	10.31	9.68	8.67
9	18.79	15.71	14.21	13.25	12.52	11.92	11.39	10.74	9.67
10	20.15	16.97	15.41	14.42	13.66	13.02	12.47	11.79	10.67
11	21.49	18.21	16.60	15.57	14.78	14.13	13.55	12.84	11.67
12	22.83	19.45	17.79	16.72	15.90	15.22	14.63	13.89	12.67
13	24.14	20.67	18.96	17.86	17.02	16.32	15.70	14.93	13.67
14	*25.45*	21.89	20.13	19.00	18.13	17.40	16.77	15.97	14.67
15	*26.75*	23.10	21.30	20.13	19.24	18.49	17.84	17.02	15.67
16	28.03	24.31	22.46	21.26	20.34	19.58	18.90	18.06	16.67
17	29.31	*25.50*	23.61	22.39	21.44	20.66	19.97	19.10	17.67
18	*30.59*	26.70	24.76	23.51	22.54	21.74	21.03	20.14	18.67
19	31.85	27.88	25.91	24.63	23.64	22.81	22.09	21.18	19.67
20	33.11	29.07	27.05	*25.74*	24.73	23.89	23.15	22.22	20.67

Expansion Factors for Expected Misstatements

Risk of Incorrect Acceptance *%*	*Factor*
1	1.90
5	1.60
10	1.50
15	1.40
20	1.30
25	1.25
30	1.20
37	1.15
50	1.10

Used with permission of AICPA

Assertions

Begin with the list of assertions below and add others you think appropriate. Then write your audit program to test those assertions.

1. Inventory physically exists.
2. Inventory is owned by the company.
3. Inventory cost properly includes freight, discounts, taxes, etc.
4. Obsolete and unsalable goods have been written off or written down.
5. The inventory value does not exceed the applicable measure of market value.
6. Inventory out on consignment is properly recorded.
7. Inventory is a current asset.
8. Inventory pledged as collateral is disclosed.

_____

_____

_____

_____

_____

_____

_____

_____

_____

_____

_____

_____

_____

_____

Program Steps

_____

_____

_____

_____

_____

_____

_____

_____

_____

_____

_____

_____

_____

_____

_____

_____

_____

_____

_____

_____

EXHIBIT 4

PEACH BLOSSOM COLOGNE COMPANY

CASH VOUCHERS FOR INVENTORY PURCHASES--2009

(with supporting materials attached)

2009 Vo. No.	VENDOR	ITEM	DISCOUNT	FREIGHT	COST	VENDOR'S INVOICE DATE	RECG REPORT DATE	DATE PAID	AMOUNT PAID
1-22	Fruit Scents, Inc Hope, Michigan	695 cases #A601- Lemon Oil	Net 30	FOB Hope	120.80 /case	1/23/09	1/22/09	2/12/09	83956
		246 cases #A603- Lemon Oil			245.60 /case				60418
		203 cases #A608- Lemon Oil			370.40 /case				75191
		1055 cases #L818- Smoothing Lotion			82.40 /case				86932
									306497
1-29	Flash Freight Co.	Freight on shipment paid by voucher #1-22	cash	- - - -	8796	1/29/09		2/16/09	8796
2-10	Fruit Juicy Perfume Co. Springfield, Missouri	410 cases #L612- Moisturizing Lotion	Net 30	FOB Chi	86.40 /case	2/5/09	2/9/09	2/26/09	35424
4-06	Fruit Juicy Perfume Co. Springfield, Missouri	400 cases #H84- 4 oz. Hand Creme	Net 30	FOB Chi	99.84 /case	5/7/09	5/12/09	5/13/09	39936
		660 cases #F60- 4 oz. Face Creme			107.52 /case				70963
									110899
6-27	Fruit Scents, Inc Hope, Michigan	200 cases #E807- L'Eau de Rose	Net 30	FOB Hope	552.80 /case	6/25/09	6/29/09	7/2/09	110560
		220 cases #R315- 4 oz. Apple Oil			226.40 /case				49808
		48 cases #R320- 2 oz. Apple Oil			332.00 /case				15936
		62 cases #Q291- 8 oz. Magnolia Oil			418.40 /case				25941
									202245
7-05	Flash Freight Co.	Freight on shipment paid by voucher #6-27 (4.00 per case)	cash	- - - -	2120	7/13/09		7/20/09	2120
7-17	Fruit Juicy Perfume Co. Springfield, Missouri	590 cases #L940- Skin Tone Lotion	Net 30	FOB Chi	86.40 /case	7/27/09	7/27/09	7/30/09	50976
		350 cases #H84- 4 oz. Hand Creme			105.60 /case				36960
		307 cases #F60- 4 oz. Face Creme			107.52 /case				33009
									120945

EXHIBIT 4

PEACH BLOSSOM COLOGNE COMPANY
CASH VOUCHERS FOR INVENTORY PURCHASES--2009
(with supporting materials attached)

Page 2

2009 Vo. No.	VENDOR	ITEM	DISCOUNT	FREIGHT	COST	VENDOR'S INVOICE DATE	REC'G REPORT DATE	DATE PAID	AMOUNT PAID
8-23	Fruit Scents, Inc	312 cases #E801- L'Eau de Pomme	Net 30	FOB Hope	552.80 /case	8/3/09	8/10/09	8/20/09	172474
	Hope, Michigan	188 cases #E802- L'Eau de Abricot			552.80 /case	-	-	-	103926
		100 cases #E803- L'Eau de Teint			552.80 /case	-	-	-	55280
		75 cases #E806- L'Eau de Citron			552.80 /case				41460
		95 cases #E804- L'Eau de Chevrefeuille			552.80 /case				52516
		80 cases #E805- L'Eau de Jasmine			552.80 /case				44224
									469880
9-14	Fruit Scents, Inc	55 cases #E803- L'Eau de Teint	Net 30	FOB Hope	552.80 /case	9/7/09	9/10/09	9/21/09	30404
	Hope, Michigan	50 cases #E806- L'Eau de Citron			552.80 /case				27640
									58044
9-27	Flash Freight Co.	Freight on shipment paid by voucher #8-23 and #9-14	cash	- - - -	3820	9/16/09		9/21/09	3820
12-23	Fruit Juicy Perfume Co.	804 cases #L940- Skin Tone Lotion	Net 30	FOB Chi	86.40 /case	12/16/09	12/17/09	1/4/10	69466
	Springfield, Missouri	900 cases #L612- Moisturizing Lotion			86.40 /case				77760
									147226
12-38	Fruit Scents, Inc	103 cases #L818- Smoothing Lotion	Net 30	FOB Hope	82.40 /case	12/28/09	12/30/09	1/8/10	8487
	Hope, Michigan								
12-42	Flash Freight Co.	Freight on shipment paid by voucher #12-38	cash	- - - -	412	12/31/09		1/11/10	412

Peach Blossom Cologne Company

Inventory

12-31-09

(Prepared by Client)

C-1

Item	Size (Ounces)	Number of Cases	Number of Bottles (24/Case)	Total Ounces	Cost per Unit	Amount Inventory	Totals
Oils							
#A601 Lemon	2	284	6816	13632	2.60/oz	35443	
#A603 Lemon	4	109	2616	10464	2.60/oz	27206	
#A608 Lemon	8	83	1992	15936	1.95/oz	31075	
#R315 Apple	4	79	1896	7584	2.40/oz	18202	
#R320 Apple	2	14	336	672	7.00/oz	4704	
#Q291 Magnolia	8	23	552	4416	2.20/oz	9715	
Total Oils:							126345
Cremes							
#H84 Hand Creme	4	511	12264	49056	4.40/btl	53962	
#F60 Face Creme	4	374	8976	35904	4.48/btl	40212	
Total Cremes							94174
Lotions							
#L612 Moisturizing	8	536.5	12876	103008	3.60/btl	64354	
#L940 Skin Tone	8	587	14088	112704	3.60/btl	50717	
#L818 Smoothing	8	631	15144	121152	3.60/btl	54518	
Total Lotions							169589
Colognes							
#E801 L'Eau de Pomme	8	32	768	6144	2.90/oz	17818	
#E802 L'Eau de Abricot	8	87	2088	16704	2.90/oz	48442	
#E803 L'Eau de Teint	8	54	1296	10368	2.90/oz	30067	
#E804 L'Eau de Chevrefeuille	8	50	1188	9504	2.90/oz	27562	
#E805 L'Eau de Jasmin	8	22	528	4224	2.90/oz	12250	
#E806 L'Eau de Citron	8	46	1104	8832	2.90/oz	25613	
#E807 L'Eau de Rose	8	87.5	2100	16800	2.90/oz	48720	
Total Colognes							210472
		3609.5	86628	547104	------	------	600580

	Peach Blossom Cologne Company				C-2	
	Inventory Observation and Test Counts					
	December 31, 2009					

Stock Number	Item	Number of Cases	Number of Bottles (24/Case)	Size of Bottle	Total Ounces	
STOREROOM:			C			
L940	Skin Tone Lotion	587 n	14088	8 oz	112704	
L612	Moisturizing Lotion	536.5n	12876	8 oz	103008	
L818	Smoothing Lotion**	631 n	15144	8 oz	121152	
E806	L'Eau de Citron Cologne	46	1104	8 oz	8832	
E807	L'Eau de Rose Cologne	87.5n	2100	8 oz	16800	
E801	L'Eau de Pomme Cologne	21	504	8 oz	4032	
E803	L'Eau de Teint Cologne	54	1296	8 oz	10368	
E802	L'Eau d'Abricot Cologne	67	1608	8 oz	12864	
F60	Face Crème	374 n	8976	4 oz	35904	
H84	Hand Creme	511 n	12264	4 oz	49056	
A608	Lemon Oil	83	1992	8 oz	15936	
A603	Lemon Oil	94 n	2256	4 oz	9024	
A601	Lemon Oil	284 n	6816	2 oz	13632	
Q291	Magnolia Oil	23	552	8 oz	4416	
R315	Apple Oil	71 n	1704	4 oz	6816	
R320	Apple Oil	14	336	2 oz	672	
E804	L'Eau de Chevrefeuille	49.5	1188	8 oz	9504	
E805	L'Eau de Jasmin Cologne	22	528	8 oz	4224	
	Storeroom Total	3555.5	85332		538944	
SHIPPING DOCK:						
E801	L'Eau de Pomme Cologne	11	264	8 oz	2112	
A603	Lemon Oil	15 n	360	4 oz	1440	
E802	L'Eau d'Abricot Cologne	20 n	480	8 oz	3840	
R315	Apple Oil	8	192	4 oz	768	
	Shipping Dock Total	54	1296		8160	
	Total Inventory	3609.5	86628		547104	

C	After testing 25 unopened cases, bottle count on vendor's label accepted on unopened cases.
n	Test counted during observation. No errors observed.
NOTE:	No obsolete or damaged inventory was observed.
**	For cutoff last receiving report #12-11 was used on 12/30/09 (103 cases of #L818 Smoothing Lotion received from Fruit Scents, Inc). That shipment included in above inventory.

Assignment #5
Property, Plant, and Equipment (Fixed Assets)

The information that follows is grouped into two categories: (1) Internal Control and (2) Substantive Audit Procedures. This information is to be used to complete the exercises.

Relevant Information

Internal Control

The following internal control questionnaire was completed by Jasper Parsons. Review this questionnaire before you write your substantive audit program. Keep in mind the six categories of control procedures: (1) segregation of functions, (2) access, (3) authorization, (4) input controls, (5) processing controls, and (6) output controls. Then try to determine potential errors that could occur.

Internal Control Questionnaire–Property, Plant, and Equipment

	Yes	No	Comments
1. Are purchases of fixed assets initiated by the purchasing agent?	√	—	
2. Are all purchases of fixed assets approved by the Board of Directors?	√	—	
3. Does the company have a policy for distinguishing between those items that are to be capitalized and those that are to be expensed as repairs and maintenance?	—	√	*Except for items authorized by board, left to discretion of bookkeeper.*
4. Are all retirements authorized by a responsible official?	√	—	*Theodore Brown*
5. Are there procedures in effect to assure that all retirements are recorded?	√	—	*Retirement work orders are used.*
6. Does the company maintain a fixed asset subsidiary ledger?	√	—	
7. Is the fixed asset subsidiary ledger reconciled to the control account periodically?	√	—	
8. Are periodic comparisons made between the fixed asset subsidiary ledger and the actual assets?	√	—	*Every three years.*

Substantive Audit Procedures

Before you begin your work on fixed assets, carefully study the prior year's working papers. For the current year, you had Don McKenna prepare two schedules, referenced D-2 and D-3, providing a detailed analysis of the additions and disposals to the fixed asset and accumulated depreciation accounts.

You also had Don prepare a computation of depreciation. This schedule is referenced D-4. Peach Blossom uses straight-line depreciation for all fixed assets. The useful life is 30 years on all buildings, 20 years on all machinery and equipment, four years on all automotive equipment, and 20 years on all furniture and fixtures. These useful lives were adopted by Peach Blossom after a joint session between their management and your audit firm several years ago. Also discussed in that meeting was the amount of depreciation to take in the year a fixed asset was acquired or disposed of. It was decided that, while it was more accurate to take depreciation for the exact number of months the assets were owned, it was more practical to take one-half year of depreciation in the year acquired and one-half year depreciation in the year of disposal. The firm has been following that policy.

With regard to additions to fixed assets, you may assume that on December 30, 2009, when you first visited the client's plant, you were given a guided tour of the facilities. You were able to move freely around the plant during the inventory observation on January 1, 2010. While walking around in the client's plant, you toured with "eyes open." After examining the additions to fixed assets schedule prepared by Don McKenna, you could recall having seen each of the fixed asset additions as you toured the client's facilities.

Don McKenna pulled from the files all cash vouchers and supporting materials for all disbursements related to fixed asset additions and repair and maintenance expense. Don summarized all the information from those vouchers in Exhibit 5. (This information is being provided to you in lieu of the actual client documents. Treat this material as though it were the actual client documents belonging to the client and not the auditor.) You may assume that all the vouchers have the appropriate supporting materials attached and that all vouchers have been approved.

With regard to the disposal of fixed assets, you may assume that the client maintains a detailed fixed asset subsidiary ledger from which you were able to obtain the cost and acquisition dates of assets retired or otherwise disposed of. You were able to agree the cost and acquisition dates of the disposal on schedule D-3 with the fixed asset subsidiary ledger. You may also assume that you traced the cash proceeds from the fixed asset disposal transaction into the cash receipts journal.

Required Exercises

1. Prepare a substantive audit program for fixed asset transactions and balances.

   The construction of a program for fixed asset transactions and balances should begin with an explicit recognition of the five financial statement assertions: (1) existence or occurrence, (2) completeness, (3) rights and obligations, (4) valuation or allocation, and (5) presentation and disclosure. From these assertions, you should derive your specific audit objectives related to fixed asset transactions and balances.

   Your audit program should address the five financial statement assertions, as well as any internal control weaknesses. In this regard, keep in mind the six categories of control procedures. You may assume that you have satisfied yourself with respect to any assertions not specifically mentioned in the narrative.

As you write your program, remember the generalized evidence-gathering procedures of (1) recalculation, (2) physical observation, (3) confirmation, (4) verbal inquiry, (5) vouching of documents, (6) tracing, (7) scanning, and (8) analytical procedures. Use them to help you write the specific evidence-gathering procedures in your program.

Use form AP-4 to write your program. Use the financial statement assertions as the major headings in your program. List the appropriate audit steps under each of these captions.

2. Prepare a summary schedule of property, plant, and equipment similar to schedule D-1 in the prior year working papers. Also complete your audit work on schedules D-2, D-3, and D-4.

A final schedule prepared for you in the fixed assets area by Don McKenna is an analysis of the Repairs and Maintenance account. This schedule is referenced D-5. Carefully examine the vouchers listed on this schedule and in Exhibit 5 to determine whether items were properly treated. Prepare any adjustments you believe are necessary.

Substantive Audit Program–Property, Plant and Equipment

Assertions

Begin with the list of assertions below and add others you think appropriate. Then write your audit program to test those assertions.

1. All recorded fixed assets are in productive use.
2. All asset disposals have been recorded.
3. All asset additions have been recorded.
4. Repair and maintenance expenses have not been capitalized.
5. Asset additions have not been charged to repairs and maintenance expense.
6. All freight, installation, taxes, etc. on additions have been capitalized.
7. Depreciation has been calculated accurately.
8. Assets pledged as collateral have not been improperly removed.

_____

_____

_____

_____

_____

_____

_____

_____

_____

_____

_____

_____

_____

_____

_____

_____

_____

_____

_____

_____

Program Steps

EXHIBIT 5

PEACH BLOSSOM COLOGNE COMPANY

CASH VOUCHERS FOR PROPERTY, PLANT, AND EQUIPMENT DISBURSEMENTS—2009

(with supporting materials attached)

2009 Vo. No.	Vendor	Item	Discount	Freight Terms	Cost	Vendor Invoice Date	Receiving Report Date	Date Paid	Amount
2-18	Barrington Construction Co. Barrington, Illinois	Repair and replace ceiling in repackaging area	Cash	- - -	4400	2/5/09	- - -	2/5/09	4400
3-25	Meyers Belts and Conveyors Gary, Indiana	Repair parts for conveyor system	Net 30	FOB Chi	3200	3/13/09	3/19/09	3/30/09	3200
5-40	Stark Equipment Michigan City, Indiana	One (1) forklift tractor	Cash	- - -	18900	5/20/09	5/21/09	5/25/09	18900
7-02	Kopel and Kopel Chicago, Illinois	Construct platforms for retrieval system and ready site for new system	Cash	- - -	3520	7/8/09	- - -	7/8/09	3520
7-12	Thompson Industrial Systems Chicago, Illinois	Installation of overhead storage and retrieval system	Net 30	- - -	178200	7/30/09	7/30/09	8/26/09	178200
8-05	Douglas Recken Construct. Chicago, Illinois	Prepare site for package labeling machine	Cash	- - -	2450	8/3/09	- - -	8/10/09	2450
8-19	Simon-Weller Mfg. Co. Gary, Indiana	Package labeling machine	Cash	- - -	8400	8/6/09	- - -	8/21/09	8400
9-08	Hart Murphy Office Outfitters Chicago, Illinois	Two (2) Itsubitsi photocopy machines	Cash	- - -	6800	9/16/09	9/16/09	9/16/09	6800
11-11	Crown Ford Chicago, Illinois	One (1) Ford sedan	Cash	- - -	19500	11/4/09	11/11/09	11/12/09	19500
12-26	Alex McBane Heating and Air Conditioning	Annual servicing of furnace and heating system	Cash	- - -	1840	12/23/09	- - -	1/5/10	1840

		Peach Blossom Cologne Company		D-2	

Peach Blossom Cologne Company
Additions to Property, Plant, and Equipment
12-31-09
(Prepared by Client)

Vo. No.	Vendor	Item Description	Cost
3-25	Meyers Belt and Conveyors Gary, IN	Repair parts for conveyor system	3200
5-40	Stark Equipment Michigan City, IN	One (1) forklift tractor	18900
7-12	Thompson Industrial Systems Chicago, IL	Installation of overhead storage and retrieval system	178200
8-19	Simon-Weller Mfg Company Gary, IN	Package labeling machine	8400
9-08	Hart-Murphy Office Outfitters Chicago, IL	Two (2) Itsubitsi photocopiers	6800
11-11	Crown Ford Chicago, IL	One (1) Ford sedan	19500
	Total additions		235000

Peach Blossom Cologne Company

Retirements of Property, Plant, and Equipment

12-31-09

(Prepared by Client)

D -3

Journal Vo. No.	Asset Description	Date Acquired	Date Sold	Depreciation Rate-Method		Cost	Accum. Deprec.	Book Value	Proceeds	Gain (Loss) on Disposal
4-23	Machinery and equipment - Forklift tractor	8-7-98	4-6-09	5%	S.L.	12500	7500	5000	500	(4500)
						12500	7500	5000	500	(4500)

100

Peach Blossom Cologne Company **D-4**

Depreciation Computation

12-31-09

(Prepared by client)

Asset	Amount	Rate	2009 Deprec. Provision	Totals
BUILDINGS:				
Held full year	276263	3.33%	9209	
Additions	----	1.67%	----	
Retirements	----	1.67%	----	9209
MACH. & EQUIPMENT:				
Held full year	540845	5.00%	27042	
Additions	208700	2.50%	5218	
Retirements	12500	2.50%	313	32573
AUTOMOTIVE :				
Held full year	99425	25.00%	24856	
Additions	19500	12.50%	4238	
Retirements	----	12.50%	----	29094
OFFICE FURN & FIXTURES:				
Held full year	106433	5.00%	5322	
Additions	6800	2.50%	170	
Retirements	----	2.50%	----	5492
				76368

Peach Blossom Cologne Company				**D-5**	
Repairs and Maintenance Account					
12-31-09					
(Prepared by client)					
Vo. No.	Vendor	Item Description		Cost	
2-18	Barrington Construction Co.	Repair and replace ceiling in repackaging area		4400	
7-2	Kopel and Kopel	Construct platforms and ready site for new overhead storage and retrieval system		3520	
8-5	Douglas Recken Construction	Prepare site for package labeling machine		2450	
12-26	Alex McBane Heat. & Air Cond.	Annual servicing of furnace & heating systems		1840	
		Vouchers less than $500 not listed		4012	
				16222	

Assignment #6
Accounts Payable Processing
and Unrecorded Liabilities

The information that follows is grouped into two categories: 1) Internal Control and 2) Substantive Audit Procedures. This information is to be used to complete the exercises for this assignment. *Do the optional exercises only if told to do so by your instructor.*

Relevant Information

Internal Control

The Peach Blossom Cologne Company uses a voucher system to make cash disbursements and also maintains an accounts payable subsidiary ledger that provides a record of the total amount owed to each vendor. Vouchers are prepared as invoices are received and are held in an unpaid voucher file (filed by payment date) until the cash is disbursed. A voucher number is a two-number code with the first number representing the month in which the voucher was recorded and the second number representing the order in which the voucher was recorded in the month. For example, 11-3 would be the voucher number for the third invoice recorded in the month of November. The following internal control questionnaire was prepared for you by Jasper Parsons. Study the questionnaire in order to analyze Peach Blossom's control over accounts payable. Parker Shelton explained to you that Dave Dull, the accounts payable clerk, made occasional errors but was improving.

While going through the questionnaire, think about the six categories of control procedures: (1) segregation of functions, (2) access, (3) authorization, (4) input controls, (5) processing controls, and (6) output controls, and consider errors or irregularities that could occur. Also review the Permanent File narrative related to accounts payable.

Typical accounts payable errors or irregularities include:

1. Purchases may have been recorded in the wrong account.
2. A liability may have been recorded for a fictitious company.
3. The purchase and liability may have been recorded in the wrong accounting period.
4. A purchase or liability may have been omitted.
5. Purchases may have been recorded but the merchandise may not have been received.

Internal Control Questionnaire–Accounts Payable Processing

		Yes	No	Comments
1.	Does the company maintain a voucher system?	√	_	
2.	Are vouchers approved by a responsible official before payment?	√	_	*Controller initials them.*
3.	Does a responsible official review the debit distribution of vouchers for proper recording?	_	√	*Occasionally controller.*
4.	Are all purchases of merchandise and services recorded In the voucher register before disbursement?	_	√	*Some invoices are run directly through cash disbursements.*
5.	Does the company maintain an accounts payable subsidiary ledger?	√	_	
6.	Is the accounts payable subsidiary ledger reconciled monthly with the accounts payable control account?	√	_	*Balancing report is printed by software.*
7.	Are vendors' monthly statements reconciled to the accounts payable subsidiary ledger?	_	√	※
8.	Do adjustments to accounts payable require the approval of a responsible official?	√	_	*Controller initials.*
9.	Are all vendors' invoices checked for proper pricing, extensions, footings, and terms?	_	√	*Occasionally.*
10.	Does the company ensure that claims for damaged merchandise are processed promptly?	_	√	
11.	Are unmatched invoices, receiving reports, and purchase orders reviewed periodically?	_	√	
12.	Are supporting documents reviewed by check signers prior to payment?	√	_	
13.	Are supporting documents stamped "cancelled" by the check signers?	√	_	*Mrs. Stockton cancels them.*
14.	Are checks mailed directly by the person signing the check and not returned to preparers?	_	√	*Mailed by accounts payable clerk.*

Having reviewed the internal control questionnaire and the permanent file material, you should now be in a position to evaluate the internal control procedures.

Substantive Audit Procedures: Accounts Payable Balances

A schedule of accounts payable due as of December 31, 2009, was prepared by Dave Dull. The schedule is referenced E-1. You requested Dave to pull from the files the cash vouchers (along with supporting materials) for all items listed in schedule E-1. He did so and summarized all the information from those vouchers for you in Exhibit 6. (The information in Exhibit 6 is being provided to you in lieu of the actual client documents. Treat this information as though it were the documents belonging to the client and not the auditor.) You may assume that all vouchers have been properly approved and have the appropriate supporting materials attached. You may assume that you traced each vouchered invoice to the accounts payable subsidiary ledger and the January cash disbursements journal and found no discrepancies.

As part of your search for unrecorded liabilities you reviewed the voucher register and cash disbursements journal for the period January 1 through January 11, 2010. You also examined the unmatched invoice and receiver file from January 1 to January 22, 2010. You may assume that none of the January disbursements from January 12 through January 22 were applicable to the year under audit; no unmatched invoices or receiving reports for the period January 1 to January 22, 2010 were applicable to 2009.

Exhibit 7 includes an excerpt from the receiving log for December showing the last receiving reports for the year. Also included in this exhibit are the voucher register for January 1 to January 11, as well as the receiving log for that same period. You should examine the transactions recorded in these two records to determine whether the company has recorded purchases of merchandise and services in the proper period. You may assume that all the information in the receiving log is correct.

You sent confirmations to Fruit Juicy Perfume Company and Fruit Scents, Inc. These confirmations are included in the working papers referenced E-3 and E-4, respectively.

Search for Other Unrecorded Liabilities

The search for unrecorded liabilities consists of a search for (1) unrecorded accounts payable and (2) a search for other unrecorded liabilities. You should perform the search for unrecorded *accounts payable* in this assignment documenting your evidence on working paper E-2. Defer the search for *other unrecorded liabilities* until Assignment #8, *Completing the Audit.*

To complete your search for *other unrecorded liabilities,* you and/or your assistant did the following:

1. Obtained a letter concerning pending litigation from the client's attorneys, Edwards, Overstreet, and Gilley. The letter is in the working papers referenced A.L./E-5. (This working paper is included in Assignment #8, *Completing the Audit.*)

2. Obtained a written representation from client management regarding liabilities and other matters. The letter is in the working papers referenced L.O.R./E-6. (This working paper is included in Assignment #8, *Completing the Audit.*)

3. Reviewed the bank confirmation for possible note liabilities or contingencies. The bank confirmation is found in the Assignment #2 working papers, referenced A-2.

4. Reviewed the minutes from meetings of the Board of Directors searching for debt authorization or other liabilities.

5. Reviewed certain operating accounts, such as interest and professional fees looking for possible unrecorded note obligations, additional litigation contingencies, etc. (Assume that you found none.)

Note that as you perform your search for other unrecorded liabilities, work performed and evidence collected in other assignments can be applicable. There may be items in other assignments (not detailed here) that relate to your search for unrecorded liabilities. Assignment #8 includes forms for preparing (1) a memorandum dealing with contingent liabilities and subsequent events (working paper E-7) and (2) other unrecorded liabilities (working paper E-8). You should wait until Assignment #8 to complete the search for other unrecorded liabilities and prepare these memos.

Exercises

PART A–Audit of Internal Control (Optional)

1. Prepare a business process flowchart for the Accounts Payable Processing system. Use form P-5 or software. The headings for this flowchart have been provided for you on this form. Remember that the Accounts Payable business process is a continuation of Inventory-Purchases. In your flowchart, show the flow of documentation, the steps involved in the process, and note any internal control features. Start with the purchasing agent's matching of the three documents (vendor's invoice, receiving report, and purchase order).

2. Analyze the control procedures (strengths) related to accounts payable processing. For each strength, describe how you could test the procedure using a test of control. Keep in mind the control procedure categories. Use form CSF-2. Classify the control procedures according to the six categories (see General Instructions and Preparations).

3. For each weakness you find, list the weakness, a possible error or irregularity that may occur because of the weakness, and a compensating substantive test of transactions or balances to detect the error or irregularity assuming the necessary records and documents are available to you. Use form CWF-2. Classify the weaknesses according to the six control procedure categories. You should keep these weaknesses in mind, as well as the financial statement assertions, as you write the substantive audit steps in your programs.

4. Prepare an audit program for the Accounts Payable business process. Your program should consist of (1) tests of controls; (2) substantive tests of details of transactions; and/or (3) dual-purpose tests having both test of controls and substantive aspects. Utilize the analysis of strengths to design your tests of controls and the analysis of the weaknesses to guide you in preparing your substantive tests of transactions, remembering to keep the financial statement assertions in mind. Write your program on form SP-2. Write the appropriate steps under the following headings in your program: Tests of Controls, Dual-Purpose Tests, and Substantive Tests of Transactions.

PART B–Required Exercises: Substantive Procedures

1. Prepare a substantive audit program for Accounts Payable Balances and Unrecorded Liabilities.

   The construction of your audit program for accounts payable balances and unrecorded liabilities should begin with an explicit recognition of the five financial statement assertions: (1) existence or occurrence, (2) completeness, (3) rights and obligations, (4) valuation or allocation, and (5) presentation and disclosure. You should derive your specific audit objectives concerning accounts payable balances and unrecorded liabilities from these assertions.

   Your audit program should address the five financial statement assertions, as well as any internal control weaknesses you have found. In this regard, keep in mind the six control procedure categories. You may assume that you have satisfied yourself as to any assertions not specifically mentioned in the narrative.

   As you write your program, remember the generalized evidence-gathering procedures of (1) recalculation, (2) physical observation, (3) confirmation, (4) verbal inquiry, (5) vouching of documents, (6) tracing, (7) scanning, and (8) analytical procedures. Use them to help you write the specific evidence-gathering procedures in your program.

   Use form AP-5 to write your program. Use the financial statement assertions as the major headings in your program and list the appropriate audit steps under each of these captions.

2. Review the prior year's working papers referenced E-1 to E-4, the Permanent File material related to accounts payable, as well as the internal control questionnaire. After reviewing this material, perform the necessary audit work on working paper E-1 and prepare a schedule similar to E-2 in the prior year's working papers. Also perform any necessary audit work on schedules E-3 and E-4. (Work on schedules E-5 through E-8 is deferred to Assignment #8, *Completing the Audit*.)

Treasurer

PEACH BLOSSOM COLOGNE COMPANY

Accounts Payable Processing

Purchasing Agent

**Accounts
Payable Clerk**

Purchasing Agent

Accounts Payable Processing
Internal Control Strengths

Strength	Possible Test of Controls

PEACH BLOSSOM COLOGNE COMPANY   **CWF-2**

Accounts Payable Processing
Internal control Weaknesses

Weakness	Potential Error	Compensating Substantive Procedure

**Accounts Payable Processing
Program**

_____
_____
_____
_____
_____
_____
_____
_____
_____
_____
_____
_____
_____
_____
_____
_____
_____
_____
_____
_____
_____
_____
_____
_____
_____
_____
_____
_____
_____
_____

Substantive Audit Program—Accounts Payable Balances and Unrecorded Liabilities

Assertions

Begin with the list of assertions below and add others you think appropriate. Then write your audit program to test those assertions.

1. All material liabilities are recorded.
2. All important contingencies are either provided for in the accounts or disclosed in footnotes.
3. Liabilities are properly classified as to their contingent or direct nature.
4. Liabilities are properly classified as to their current or long-term status.

_____

_____

_____

_____

_____

_____

_____

_____

_____

_____

_____

_____

_____

_____

_____

_____

_____

_____

Program Steps

EXHIBIT 6

PEACH BLOSSOM COLOGNE COMPANY

CASH VOUCHERS FOR ACCOUNTS PAYABLE--2009

(with supporting materials attached)

2009	Vendor	Item	Discount	Freight Terms	Cost	Vendor Invoice Date	Receiving Report Date	Date Paid	Amount
12-08	Hammel, Hammel & Johnson Advertising Agency	Advertising transactions	Net 30	- - -	5740	12/7/09	- - -	1/4/10	5740
12-16	Norton Exterminators	Pest control	Net 30	- - -	445	12/16/09	- - -	1/4/10	445
12-20	Edwards, Overstreet & Gilley	Retainer and legal fees	Net 30	- - -	8700	12/17/09	- - -	1/4/10	8700
12-23	Fruit Juicy Perfume Co.	See voucher in inventory section				12/16/09	12/17/09	1/4/10	147226
12-26	Alex McBane Heating & Air Conditioning	See voucher in property, plant, and equipment section				12/23/09	- - -	1/5/10	1840
12-34	Barrows Office Supply	Office supplies	Net 30	- - -	1590	12/18/09	- - -	1/5/10	1590
12-36	Kalvin & Hubbs Consulting	Consulting engagement	Net 30	- - -	2350	12/28/09	- - -	1/6/10	2350
12-38	Fruit Scents, Inc.	See voucher in inventory section				12/28/09	12/30/09	1/8/10	8487
12-42	Flash Freight Co.	See voucher in inventory section				12/31/09	- - -	1/11/10	412

EXHIBIT 7

PEACH BLOSSOM COLOGNE COMPANY
Receiving Log
December 2009

Date Shipped	Receiving Date	Receiver No.	Vendor	Description	Terms
12/12/09	12/17/09	12-10	Fruit Juicy Perfume Co.	804 cases Skin Tone Lotion 900 cases Moisturizing Lotion	FOB, Chi
12/26/09	12/30/09	12-11	Fruit Scents, Inc.	103 cases Smoothing Lotion	FOB, Hope

PEACH BLOSSOM COLOGNE COMPANY
Receiving Log
January 2010

Date Shipped	Receiving Date	Receiver No.	Vendor	Description	Terms	
12/30/09	1/4/10	1-01	Fruit Juicy Perfume Co.	75 cases Face Cream	FOB, Chi	Destin Jan
12/31/09	1/6/10	1-02	Fruit Juicy Perfume Co.	45 cases Moisturizing Lotion	FOB, Chi	Destin @ Jan Shippin Jan
12/31/09	1/7/10	1-03	Fruit Scents, Inc.	85 cases L'Eau de Pomme Cologne	FOB, Hope	Dec

115

EXHIBIT 7 (Continued)

PEACH BLOSSOM COLOGNE COMPANY
Voucher Register
January 2010
(selected portions)

Date	Voucher No.	Name	Explanation	Acct #	Amount	
1/4/10	1-1	Central Power & Light	Electric service 11/26 to 12/24	830	1400	∪
1/4/10	1-2	William F. Reimann	Truck repairs	828	468	
1/4/10	1-3	Fruit Juicy Perfume Co.	Receiver No. 1-01	109	8064	
1/4/10	1-4	Hoffmann Supply Co.	Conveyor belts	828	240	
1/6/10	1-5	Fruit Juicy Perfume Co.	Receiver No. 1-02	109	3888	
1/6/10	1-6	A to Z Janitorial	Services for December	832	365	7
1/6/10	1-7	Flash Freight Co.	Freight for merchandise on rec. 1-03 for invoice dated 12/31/09	109	340	8
1/6/10	1-8	Fulton Paper Co.	Copying paper	824	275	
1/7/10	1-9	Fruit Scents, Inc.	Receiver No. 1-03	109	46988	5
1/8/10	1-10	Steck Hamilton Office Supplies	Office supplies	824	1214	
1/11/10	1-11	Petrozine Fuel Co.	Fuel oil	830	786	

Assignment #7
Notes Payable and Accrued Interest

The information that follows is grouped into two categories: (1) Internal Control and (2) Substantive Audit Procedures. This information is to be used to complete the exercises.

Relevant Information

Internal Control

The following internal control questionnaire was completed by Jasper Parsons on December 15, 2009. Review this questionnaire before you write your audit program for notes payable related transactions and balances. As you go through the questionnaire, keep in mind the six categories of control procedures: (1) segregation of functions, (2) access, (3) authorization, (4) input controls, (5) processing controls, and (6) output controls. Then try to think of potential errors or irregularities that could occur.

Internal Control Questionnaire–Notes Payable and Accrued Interest

		Yes	No	Comments
1.	Is specific authority to obligate the company separated from the actual recording of debt transactions?	√	_	*Treasurer has authority to obligate. Controller records.*
2.	Are all borrowings authorized by the board of directors?	√	_	
3.	Are paid notes cancelled and stamped "paid?"	√	_	
4.	Are detailed records of borrowings maintained by an employee who is not authorized to sign checks or notes?	√	_	*Kept by Don McKenna.*
5.	Does the accounting department review accruals of interest on all debt instruments?	√	_	
6.	Are interest payments reconciled with notes on hand?	_	√	

Substantive Audit Procedures: Notes Payable And Accrued Interest

Study the notes payable and accrued interest schedule included in the prior year's working papers. That schedule is referenced F-1. At December 31, 2009, Peach Blossom Cologne Company had a note payable outstanding to the Midwestern Mutual Life Insurance Company in the amount of $150,000. You have received a confirmation of the note and terms from Midwestern. The confirmation is included in the working papers, referenced F-2. You may assume that the data in this confirmation agrees with the client's copy of the note, which you have examined. You may assume that you have traced the proceeds from the note into the cash receipts journal.

For the $125,000 note to Big City National, you were able to trace the $140,938 payment for principal and interest into the cash disbursements journal dated April 30, 2009 (voucher 4-38). You should review the prior year's bank confirmation, working paper A-2, and the notes payable working paper F-1 for verification of the information pertaining to this note.

The only assets subject to lien with respect to the long-term debt are those indicated in the confirmation. Peach Blossom has made no provision for funding the long-term debt.

Required Exercises

1. Prepare a substantive audit program for Notes Payable and Accrued Interest.

   The construction of an audit program for notes payable transactions and balances should begin with the auditor's explicit recognition of the five financial statement assertions: (1) existence or occurrence, (2) completeness, (3) rights and obligations, (4) valuation or allocation, and (5) presentation and disclosure. You should derive your specific audit objectives for notes payable and accrued interest from these assertions.

   Your audit program should address the five financial statement assertions, as well as any internal control weaknesses. In this regard, keep in mind the six categories of control procedures. You may assume that you have satisfied yourself as to any assertions not specifically mentioned in the narrative.

   As you write your program, remember the generalized evidence-gathering procedures of (1) recalculation, (2) physical observation, (3) confirmation, (4) verbal inquiry, (5) vouching of documents, (6) tracing, (7) scanning, and (8) analytical procedures. Use them to help you write the specific evidence-gathering procedures in your program.

   Use form AP-6 to write your program. Use the financial statement assertions as your program headings. List the appropriate audit steps under each of these captions.

2. Prepare a schedule similar to schedule F-1 for the current year, performing all required audit work. Also make any notations on F-2 that you deem necessary.

Substantive Audit Program—Notes Payable and Accrued Interest

Assertions

Begin with the list of assertions below and add others you think appropriate. Then write your audit program to test those assertions.

1. All material debt liabilities are recorded.
2. Debt liabilities are properly classified as to their contingent or direct nature.
3. Debt liabilities are properly classified as to their current or long-term status.
4. Terms, conditions, and restrictions relating to debt are adequately disclosed.

_____

_____

_____

_____

_____

_____

_____

_____

_____

_____

_____

_____

_____

_____

_____

_____

_____

_____

_____

_____

_____

_____

_____

_____

Program Steps

MIDWESTERN MUTUAL LIFE INSURANCE COMPANY
834 O'Keefe Street
Chicago, Illinois 60614

January 19, 2010
Anderson, Olds and Watershed
Certified Public Accountants
615 Big City National Bank Building
Main at Michigan Avenue
Chicago, Illinois 60612

At the request of Mr. Parker Shelton of the Peach Blossom Cologne Company, we confirm to you that the company was indebted to us on December 31, 2009 in the following manner:

> Note dated May 31, 2009: Principal amount of $150,000 due May 31, 2019.
> Interest at 10 ½ % payable on May 31st of each year. The note is secured by plant
> machinery and equipment as listed in chattel mortgage dated May 31, 2009.

Please let us know if we can be of further assistance.

Sincerely,
William H. McHale
William H. McHale
Loan Officer

WHM/caw

Assignment #8
Completing the Audit

In every audit engagement, the reputation of your audit firm is on the line. It is therefore extremely important that you, as the auditor-in-charge, assure that the audit has been performed with the utmost care, that no material misstatements remain, and that the financial statements are materially correct in all respects. Auditing textbooks are replete with accounts of auditors who were successfully sued because they failed to follow up on unusual items discovered during the audit. The audit completion phase is the last opportunity to tie up loose ends. To complete the audit, a number of miscellaneous items remain. Use the information provided to complete the exercises in this assignment. *Do the optional exercises only if told to do so by your instructor.*

Operating Accounts

Many of the operations accounts have been examined during your completion of Assignments #2 through #7. For example, depreciation expense was tested in the fixed assets work (Assignment #5), while interest expense was examined in Assignment #7, and so forth. You may assume that all operations accounts not examined by you during your completion of Assignments #2 through #7 (e.g., Sales and Cost of Sales, etc.) have been examined by an assistant working on the Peach Blossom Cologne Company audit under your supervision. The assistant examined the accounts for unusual items, significant monthly trends, and so on. You may assume that the work revealed no items of an unusual nature and no proposed adjustments. You are satisfied that your assistant performed an adequate investigation of those accounts.

Analytical Procedures

Auditing standards require the auditor to perform analytical procedures at the end of the audit to provide an overall review of the financial information and to determine the effect of audit adjustments on the comparisons and ratios. Assume you performed this analysis and determined that the effect of your adjustments did not have a significant impact on the premises used for planning the engagement.

Required Exercises

1. **Federal Income Tax and Retained Earnings Working Papers**

   To determine the federal income taxes payable, apply the tax rate to net income before taxes (after audit adjustments). You may assume that there are no differences between tax income and accounting income. The following tax rates are applicable:

   On first $50,000 of income ....rate is 15%
   On next $25,000 of income..rate is 25%
   On income over $75,000 ....rate is 34%

   Study schedule G-1 in the prior year's working papers. Donald McKenna has prepared a similar schedule referenced G-1 for the current year. You may assume that you were able to trace all payments and deposits against the client's tax liability to the cash disbursements journal. You also examined each of the paid vouchers and were able to agree the amounts paid during 2008 and 2009 with the client's copy of the tax return. All the client's tax returns are prepared by your audit firm.

Required. After posting your adjusting entries to the working trial balance, determine the addition to or reduction of the federal income taxes recorded by the client. Perform all required audit work on schedule G-1 for the current year. Then post any required adjusting entry for income taxes to the trial balance.

Examine schedule H-1 in the prior year's working papers before preparing a similar schedule for the current year.

Required. Complete the retained earnings schedule (H-1). To obtain the ending balance of Retained Earnings *per client*: use the figures found on the working trial balance (TB-BS). Using the amounts before audit adjustments, start with the beginning balance of Retained Earnings at January 1, 2009, then subtract dividends, and add net income. To obtain the ending balance of retained earnings *per audit*: adjust the ending balance per client for the net effect of your audit adjustments as found in the totals of the "Adjustments" column on TB-IS.

2. Working Trial Balance

Required. All audit adjustments should be posted to the schedule of adjusting journal entries, working paper AJE, as well as the working trial balances, working papers TB-BS and TB-IS. Each adjustment should also be documented on the working paper that gave rise to it. After posting all adjustments, add across to obtain the trial balance per audit. Any reclassification entries affecting financial statement presentation should be posted to working paper RJE and to the trial balance. After posting these adjustments to the trial balance, add across.

3. Minutes from Meetings of Board of Directors

Excerpts of minutes of meetings of the Board of Directors are provided in the Permanent File working papers.

Required. Examine the cross-referencing on the prior year's minutes. Items of accounting import should be similarly referenced to appropriate places in the current year's working papers. The excerpts from the minutes of Board meetings should remain as part of the Permanent File located immediately after the chart of accounts.

4. Assembling the Working Papers

Required. After you have completed all your audit work, assemble your working papers in the following order:

Current File

(1) Senior's Audit Memorandum (an optional assignment)
(2) Planning working papers (from Assignment #1)
(3) Drafts of audit reports (optional assignments)
(4) Draft of financial statements and footnotes (an optional assignment)
(5) Internal control letter to management and the audit committee (an optional assignment)
(6) Working trial balances–balance sheet and income statement
(7) Schedule of adjusting journal entries
(8) Assignment working papers in working paper order (A, B, C, etc.); include internal control

analysis (if applicable) and audit program(s) with the assignment's working papers.

Permanent File

(1) History and Background
(2) Organization Chart and Organizational Structure
(3) Flowcharts (optional assignments)
(4) Internal Control Narratives
(5) Chart of Accounts
(6) Minutes of Meetings of Board of Directors.

After you have assembled your working papers in the file folder, review them a final time for cleaning up last minute details like cross-referencing, tying out, and completing explanations. Finally, turn your working papers in for the partner's review.

Optional Exercises

1. Attorney's Letter

You have requested and received from the client's attorneys a statement regarding pending litigation, contingent liabilities, and major transactions (present or planned).

Required. You should consider the information provided in this letter and incorporate it into your audit documentation. File this letter in the liabilities working papers referenced A.L./E-5.

2. Client's Letter of Representations

This letter covers the client's representations to your audit firm as to asset valuation, the status of liabilities, and other matters that may affect the financial statements.

Required. Complete the client's letter of representations by filling in dollar amounts on your firm's standard representation letter form. After having Larry Lancaster and Parker Shelton review and sign the letter, file it in the working papers section with the liabilities working papers, referenced L.O.R./E-6.

3. Contingent Liabilities and Subsequent Events Memorandum

To insure proper disclosure, you should perform a search for contingent liabilities and subsequent events. You received a letter from the client's legal counsel; this letter provides information about contingencies. You also made inquiries of the president, controller, and treasurer. Your discussions with management revealed no additional contingencies or subsequent events.

Required. You should determine from the minutes of the Board of Directors' meetings and from other evidence available to you whether all contingent liabilities and subsequent events are properly treated. After completing your investigation, prepare a memorandum documenting your findings and conclusions. A form for that memorandum is provided and referenced E-7. This memorandum should be filed with the liabilities working papers. (Note that the audit opinion may have to be modified for material contingencies. Adjustments and/or disclosures may be required; assume that the client will adjust/disclose as you propose.)

4. Unrecorded Liability Search Memorandum

Required. Having completed your evidence-gathering activities for the audit, you should prepare a memorandum documenting your search for unrecorded liabilities. A form for that memo is provided in this assignment, referenced E-8. Include this memorandum with the accrued liabilities working papers.

5. Auditor's Report on Financial Statements

Required. Prepare a draft of the auditor's report on Peach Blossom's financial statements taking into account all information obtained from your audit work. Place the draft of the audit report immediately following the planning working papers from Assignment #1.

6. Auditor's Report on Internal Control Over Financial Reporting

Review management's 2009 report on internal control over financial reporting. Also review the internal control questionnaires, as well as any work you may have done on the optional internal control audit exercises in Assignments #3 and #6.

Required. Prepare a draft of the auditor's report on internal control over financial reporting taking into account all information on Peach Blossom's internal control obtained from your audit work. Also place any required audit notations on management's report on internal control. Keep in mind that material weaknesses preclude an unqualified opinion on internal control. Put the draft of the audit report immediately following the planning working papers from Assignment #1.

7. Financial Statements and Accompanying Notes

Required. On the working trial balance, summarize and reclassify items for financial statement presentation. Prepare a draft of the current year's financial statements, including footnote disclosures. When you assemble the final working paper folder, place your draft of the financial statements immediately following the auditor's report.

8. Senior's Audit Memorandum

As the senior auditor "in-charge" in the field, you are responsible for preparing an internal memorandum discussing problems that may have a significant financial and/or economic impact on the client's statements. Discuss any significant audit and/or accounting problems you encountered, how you resolved those problems (e.g., proposed an adjustment, disclosed the item, prepared an internal control letter item, etc.), and your conclusions about the audit as a whole. This memorandum is used by the partner-in-charge as a starting point for reviewing the audit working papers.

Required. Prepare the senior's audit memorandum describing any significant problems encountered during the audit. Address this memorandum to the partner-in-charge of the Peach Blossom audit.

9. Internal Control Letter to Management and the Audit Committee

PCAOB Auditing Standard 2 requires the auditor to communicate in writing to management and to the Audit Committee of the Board of Directors all *significant deficiencies* and *material weaknesses* in internal control. In addition, the auditor is required to communicate in writing to management all *deficiencies* in internal control that are not considered significant deficiencies or material weaknesses.

Required. Prepare a letter to the Audit Committee of the Board of Directors and to management describing any deficiencies, significant deficiencies, and/or material weaknesses in internal control over financial reporting as of December 31, 2009. You should describe each deficiency or weakness and provide recommendations at to how the situation or item should be corrected. Your letter should include definitions of control deficiencies, significant deficiencies, and material weaknesses, and clearly identify the category to which each item relates. Additionally, your letter should state that the communication is intended solely for the information and use of the Board of Directors, Audit Committee, management and others within the company. Place this letter in the working papers after the draft of the financial statements and footnotes.

Peach Blossom Cologne Company				G-1	
Federal Income Taxes Payable					
12-31-09					
(Prepared by client)					
				Tax Liability	Tax Expense
Balance 12-31-08				23023	
Additions: 2009 taxes				100000	100000
Payments:				123023	
Final payment Jan. 2009 on 2008 taxes			23023		
First quarter deposit, 2009 taxes			25000		
Second quarter deposit, 2009 taxes			25000		
Third quarter deposit, 2009 taxes			25000	98023	
				25000	100000

Edwards, Overstreet, and Gilley
Attorneys at Law
1604 South Fourth . Chicago, Illinois 60614
Phone: 312-555-3892
Fax: 312-555-9998

January 20, 2010

Anderson, Olds and Watershed
Certified Public Accountants
615 Big City National Bank Building
Main at Michigan Avenue
Chicago, Illinois 60612

Re: Peach Blossom Cologne Company

Dear Sir or Madam:

By letter dated January 4, 2010, Mr. Lawrence Lancaster of Peach Blossom Cologne Company (The "Company") has requested us to furnish you with certain information in connection with your examination of the accounts of the Company as of December 31, 2009. While this firm represents the Company on a regular basis, our engagement has been limited to specific matters as to which we were consulted by the Company.

Subject to the foregoing and to the last paragraph of this letter we advise you that since January 1, 2009 we have not been engaged to give substantive attention to, or represent the Company in connection with material loss contingencies coming within the scope of clause (a) of Paragraph 5 of the Statement of Policy referred to in the last paragraph of this letter.

We are responding to an action that has been initiated against Peach Blossom Cologne Company alleging injury due to defective products. The action, *Ersham v. Peach Blossom Cologne Company,* is not yet in litigation. Investigation, preparation, including development of the factual data and legal research and progress of the matter have reached a stage whereby an assessment can be made, taking all relevant factors into account that may affect the outcome. Although the litigation is being defended vigorously and the Company has meritorious defenses, we are of the opinion that the plaintiff will likely prevail in this action, and it is extremely doubtful that the Company will prevail. As to the amount of potential loss, total costs and damages that might ultimately be assessed against the Company will be much less than the $100,000 damages claimed by the plaintiff. However, at this time the amount is not susceptible of reasonable estimation.

(Continued)

Page Two

The information set forth herein is as of the date of this letter and we disclaim any undertaking to advise you of changes which thereafter may be brought to our attention.

This response is limited by, and in accordance with, the ABA Statement of Policy Regarding Lawyers' Responses to Auditors' Requests for Information (December 1975); without limiting the generality of the foregoing, the limitation set forth in such Statement on the scope and use of this response (Paragraphs 2 and 7) are specifically incorporated herein by reference, and any description herein of any "loss contingencies" is qualified in its entirety by Paragraph 5 of the Statement and the accompanying Commentary (which is an integral part of the Statement).

Consistent with the last sentence of Paragraph 6 of the ABA Statement of Policy and pursuant to the Company's request, this will confirm as correct the Company's understanding as set forth in its audit inquiry letter to us that whenever, in the course of performing legal services for the Company with respect to a matter recognized to involve an unasserted possible claim or assessment that may call for financial statement disclosure, we have formed a professional conclusion that the Company must disclose or consider disclosure concerning such possible claim or assessment, we, as a matter of professional responsibility to the Company, will so advise the Company and will consult with the Company concerning the question of such disclosure and the applicable requirements of Statement of Financial Accounting Standards No. 5.

Very truly yours,

EDWARDS, OVERSTREET AND GILLEY

Michael Overstreet
Michael Overstreet
Partner

Peach Blossom Cologne Company

1308 Beehive Boulevard Chicago, Illinois 60615
Phone: 312-477-7288
Fax: 312-477-9999
Internet: www.peachblossom.com

February 5, 2010

Anderson, Olds and Watershed
Certified Public Accountants
615 Big City National Bank Building
Main at Michigan
Chicago, Illinois 60612

The following representations are made to you in connection with your examination of the financial statements of Peach Blossom Cologne Company as of December 31, 2009 for the purpose of expressing an opinion as to whether the financial statements present fairly, in all material respects, the financial position, results of operations, and cash flows of Peach Blossom Cologne Company in conformity with generally accepted accounting principles.

We confirm that we are responsible for the statement of financial position, results of operations, and cash flows in conformity with generally accepted accounting principles. Certain representations in this letter are described as being limited to matters that are material. Items are considered material, regardless of size, if they involve an omission or misstatement of accounting information that, in the light of surrounding circumstances, makes it probable that the judgment of a reasonable person relying on the information would be changed or influenced by the omission or misstatement.

We further confirm that the following representations made to you during your audit examination are accurate to the best of our knowledge and belief:

Financial Statements
The financial statements referred to above are fairly presented in conformity with generally accepted accounting principles. All material transactions have been properly recorded in the accounting records underlying the financial statements. No fraud exists involving management or employees who have significant roles in internal control or others that could have a material effect on the financial statements. No shortages or irregularities have been discovered that have not been disclosed to you, and to our knowledge there is nothing reflecting upon the honesty of members of our organization. The company has no plans that could materially affect the carrying value or classification of assets or liabilities.

Page Two

Receivables
Trade Accounts receivable, net, in the amount of $_____ are valid receivables and do not include any amounts for goods shipped on consignment or approval. In our opinion, the balance in Allowance for Bad Debts of $_____is sufficient to cover any losses, discounts, or allowances that may be incurred or allowed in the collection of the receivables.

Inventories:
The Company's inventory in the amount of $_____ as determined by actual count by competent employees under the supervision of management as of December 31, 2009 are fairly stated on the first-in, first-out, lower-of-cost-or-market basis. Reasonable allowance has been made for slow-moving, obsolete, unsaleable, or unusable items. All inventories are the property of the Company. Inventory balances do not include (1) amounts of goods consigned to the Company, (2) merchandise billed to customers on or before the inventory date, or (3) any items for which the liability has not been provided on the books.

Property, Plant, and Equipment:
Property, plant and equipment is owned with satisfactory title. Capitalizable charges and purchased additions during the year are stated at cost. Property disposed of or abandoned was removed from the accounts. The provision for depreciation in the amount of $_____was determined on a basis consistent with preceding years. In our opinion, depreciation methods used and depreciable lives assigned are appropriate for allocating the cost of the assets over their useful lives. The valuation account, accumulated depreciation (balance of _____) , is reasonably adequate to state property, plant, and equipment assets at a reasonable book value with respect to the utilization expected over their remaining lives.

Owned Assets:
The Company had satisfactory title to all owned assets at December 31, 2009. All significant mortgages, assignments, pledges, or other encumbrances of assets have been disclosed to you.

Liabilities:
With the possible exception of a few minor amounts, all direct liabilities of the Company amount to $_____and were recorded on the books as of December 31, 2009.

There are no:
a. Violations or possible violations of laws or regulations whose effects should be considered for disclosure in the financial statements or as a basis for recording a loss contingency.
b. Unasserted claims or assessments that our lawyer has advised us are probable of assertion and must be disclosed in accordance with FASB Statement No. 5, Accounting for Contingencies.

Page Three

    c. Other liabilities or gain or loss contingencies that are required to be accrued or disclosed by FASB Statement No. 5.

The Company had no other contingent or possible liabilities that have not been disclosed to you.

Purchase and Sales Commitments:
At December 31, 2009, the Company had no important unfilled contracts for purchases in excess of normal requirements or at prices substantially in excess of market, or for sales at prices that are expected to result in a loss.

Capital Stock:
All capital stock issued or reserved for options, warrants, or other future issuance is disclosed in the financial statements.

Minutes:
We have made available to you (1) all financial records and related data, and (2) minutes of the meetings of stockholders, directors, and committees of directors, or summaries of actions of recent meetings for which minutes have not yet been prepared. Minutes of such meetings as exhibited to you are complete and authentic records of all such meetings held during the period from January 1, 2009 through December 31, 2009.

General:
No events have occurred and no facts have been discovered since December 31, 2009, which would make the balance sheet at that date or the statement of earnings for the year then ended materially inaccurate or misleading.

No charges are pending against the Company for alleged violations of federal, state, or local laws, which would have any material effect on the financial statements. No communications from regulatory agencies have been received concerning noncompliance with or deficiencies in financial reporting practices.

The company has complied with all aspects of contractual agreements that would have a material effect on the financial statements in the event of noncompliance.

No director, officer, or principal holder of the Company's equity securities was indebted (except for minor amounts for ordinary travel and expenses) to the Company at any time during the year.

The following have been properly recorded or disclosed in the financial statements:
    a. Related-party transactions, including sales, purchases, loans, transfers, leasing arrangements,

Page Four

      and guarantees, and amounts receivable from or payable to related parties.

b. Guarantees, whether written or oral, under which the company is contingently liable.

c. Significant estimates and material concentrations known to management that are required to be disclosed in accordance with the AICPA's Statement of Position 94-6 (Disclosure of Certain Significant Risks and Uncertainties). (Significant estimates are estimates at the balance sheet date that could change materially within the next year; concentrations refer to volumes of business, revenues, available sources of supply, or markets or geographic areas for which events could occur that would significantly disrupt normal finances within the next year.)

Internal Control:

We confirm that we are responsible for establishing and maintaining adequate internal control over financial reporting. We have prepared a separate report on internal control over financial reporting in compliance with section 404 of the Sarbanes-Oxley Act of 2002.

Very truly yours,

Lawrence Lancaster
President
Peach Blossom Cologne Company

Parker Shelton
Controller
Peach Blossom Cologne Company

_____
_____
_____
_____
_____
_____
_____
_____
_____
_____
_____
_____
_____
_____
_____
_____
_____
_____
_____
_____
_____
_____
_____
_____
_____
_____
_____
_____
_____
_____

Peach Blossom Cologne Company

1308 Bee Hive Boulevard Chicago, Illinois 60615
Phone: 312-477-7288
Fax: 312-477-9999
Internet: www.peachblossom.com

February 4, 2010

Anderson, Olds and Watershed
Certified Public Accountants
615 Big City National Bank Building
Main at Michigan
Chicago, Illinois 60612

Our management is responsible for establishing and maintaining adequate internal control over financial reporting. Under the supervision and with the participation of our management, including our principal executive officer and principal financial officer, we conducted an evaluation of the effectiveness of our internal control over financial reporting based on the framework in *Internal Control–Integrated Framework* issued by the Committee of Sponsoring Organizations of the Treadway Commission (the COSO criteria). Based on our evaluation under the COSO criteria, our management concluded that our internal control over financial reporting was effective as of December 31, 2009. Our management's assessment of the effectiveness of our internal control over financial reporting as of December 31, 2009 has been audited by Anderson, Olds and Watershed, an independent registered public accounting firm, as stated in their report which is included herein.

Lawrence Lancaster
President
Peach Blossom Cologne Company

Parker Shelton
Controller
Peach Blossom Cologne Company

IV
Current Year's
Working Trial Balance

Peach Blossom Cologne Company
Working Trial Balance-Balance Sheet
12-31-09

TB-BS

	Working Paper Reference	Per Audit 12-31-08	Per Books 12-31-09	Adjustments Debit	Adjustments Credit	Per Audit 12-31-09	Reclassification Items Debit	Reclassification Items Credit	Financial Statements 12-31-09
Assets:									
101 Cash-Big City National Bank		339415	420678						
105 Accounts receivable		124021	235380						
106 Allowance for bad debts		(10485)	(4800)						
109 Inventory		777152	600580						
210 Land		82250	82250						
220 Buildings		276263	276263						
221 Accum. depn.- buildings		(65416)	(74625)						
230 Machinery and equipment		540845	737045						
231 Accum. depn.- mach.& equip.		(160866)	(185939)						
240 Automotive equipment		99425	118925						
241 Accum. depn.- auto. equip.		(52798)	(81892)						
250 Office furniture & fixtures		106433	113233						
251 Accum. depn.- off. furn.& fix.		(37581)	(43073)						
Total assets		2018658	2194025						
Liabilities:									
301 Accounts payable		223161	176790						
305 Accrued interest		10625	8750						
306 Dividends payable		15725	15725						
307 Federal income tax payable		23023	25000						
308 Notes payable-short term		125000							
401 Notes payable-long term			150000						
Total liabilities		397534	376265						
Owners' Equity:									
501 Common stock		925000	925000						
505 Other contributed capital		95979	95979						
601 Retained earnings		429855	600145						
605 Dividends		(15725)	(15725)						
610 Current net income		186015	212361						
Total owners' equity		1621124	1817760						
Total liabilities & owners' equity		2018658	2194025						

Peach Blossom Cologne Company
Working Trial Balance-Income Statement
12-31-09

TB-IS

	Working Paper Reference	Per Audit 12-31-08	Per Books 12-31-09	Adjustments Debit	Adjustments Credit	Per Audit 12-31-09	Reclassification Items Debit	Reclassification Items Credit	Financial Statements 12-31-09
REVENUE:									
701 Sales		3447472	3857549						
703 Sales Returns & Allowances		(26530)	(28318)						
Net Sales		3420942	3829231						
EXPENSES:									
801 Cost of Goods Sold		1420933	1651366						
Gross Margin		2000009	2177865						
OPERATING EXPENSES:									
820 Wage and Salary Expense		1418720	1487700						
821 Payroll Tax Expense		99310	105924						
822 Depreciation Expense		64422	76368						
823 Rent Expense		3750	3750						
824 Office Supplies Expense		8615	10825						
825 Small Tools Expense		2988	5650						
826 Advertising Expense		6313	7980						
827 Insurance		15737	22415						
828 Repairs and Maintenance		17869	16222						
829 Property Tax		13463	17100						
830 Utilities		10670	14325						
831 Professional Fees		26875	35875						
832 Miscellaneous Expense		302	1771						
833 Provision for Bad Debts		9925	8650						
834 Freight Expense		28150	32386						
Total Operating Expenses		1727109	1846941						
Net Income From Operations		272900	330924						
OTHER INCOME (EXPENSE):									
901 Interest Expense		(27500)	(14063)						
930 Gain(Loss)Sale of Fixed Assets		18638	(4500)						
950 Miscellaneous Income		0	0						
Net Other Income		(8862)	(18563)						
Net Income Before Taxes		264038	312361						
940 Federal Income Tax		78023	100000						
Net Income		186015	212361						

V
Prior Year's Working Papers

PEACH BLOSSOM COLOGNE COMPANY
Senior's Audit Memorandum
December 31, 2008

To: Partner-in-Charge
Peach Blossom Cologne Company Audit

As senior-in-charge of the audit examination of the financial statements of Peach Blossom Cologne Company for the year ended December 31, 2008, I have prepared all accompanying working papers in accordance with generally accepted auditing standards and included all procedures considered necessary in the circumstances. I have performed all steps of the audit program. Other than those described in the following paragraphs, there were no special accounting or auditing problems encountered.

When searching for unrecorded liabilities, I discovered that the Company had not recorded a December utility invoice. I proposed an adjusting entry to record the $2,025 liability. Moreover, the Company had incorrectly extended inventory, for which I proposed a $2,650 adjustment.

The Company is liable to Big City National Bank for an unsecured note in the amount of $125,000. The note, which is due April 30, 2009, has been disclosed in the footnotes. No contingent liabilities were observed.

It is my opinion that the accompanying draft of the client's financial statements is in accordance with generally accepted accounting principles with proper disclosure and that we may issue the unqualified opinion as shown in the accompanying draft of the audit report.

Jasper W. Parsons
Audit Senior
February 9, 2009

ANDERSON, OLDS, & WATERSHED

Certified Public Accountants
615 Big City National Bank Building
Main at Michigan Avenue
Chicago, Illinois 60612
Phone: (312) 555-4452
Fax: (312) 555-9991
www.aowcpa.com

REPORT OF INDEPENDENT REGISTERED PUBLIC ACCOUNTING FIRM

Board of Directors and Stockholders
The Peach Blossom Cologne Company

We have audited the accompanying balance sheets of Peach Blossom Cologne Company, Inc. as of December 31, 2008 and 2007, and the related statements of income, changes in shareholders' equity, and cash flows for the years then ended. These financial statements are the responsibility of the Company's management. Our responsibility is to express an opinion on these financial statements based on our audits.

We conducted our audits in accordance with auditing standards of the Public Company Accounting Oversight Board (United States). Those standards require that we plan and perform the audit to obtain reasonable assurance about whether the financial statements are free of material misstatement. An audit includes examining, on a test basis, evidence supporting the amounts and disclosures in the financial statements. An audit also includes assessing the accounting principles used and significant estimates made by management, as well as evaluating the overall financial statement presentation. We believe that our audits provide a reasonable basis for our opinion.

In our opinion, the financial statements referred to above present fairly, in all material respects, the financial position of Peach Blossom Cologne Company as of December 31, 2008 and 2007, and the results of its operations and its cash flows for the years then ended in conformity with accounting principles generally accepted in the United States.

We have also audited, in accordance with the standards of the Public Company Accounting Oversight Board (United States), the effectiveness of Peach Blossom Cologne Company's internal control over financial reporting as of December 31, 2008, based on criteria established in *Internal Control—Integrated Framework* issued by the Committee of Sponsoring Organizations of the Treadway Commission and our report dated February 9, 2009, expressed an unqualified opinion thereon.

Anderson, Olds, and Watershed

Certified Public Accountants
February 9, 2009

ANDERSON, OLDS, & WATERSHED

Certified Public Accountants
615 Big City National Bank Building
Main at Michigan Avenue
Chicago, Illinois 60612
Phone: (312) 555-4452
Fax: (312) 555-9991
www.aowcpa.com

REPORT OF INDEPENDENT REGISTERED PUBLIC ACCOUNTING FIRM ON INTERNAL CONTROL OVER FINANCIAL REPORTING

Board of Directors and Stockholders
The Peach Blossom Cologne Company

We have audited management's assessment, included in the accompanying Report of Management on Internal Control Over Financial Reporting that Peach Blossom Cologne Company maintained effective internal control over financial reporting as of December 31, 2008, based on criteria established in *Internal Control— Integrated Framework* issued by the Committee of Sponsoring Organizations of the Treadway Commission (the COSO criteria). Peach Blossom Cologne Company's management is responsible for maintaining effective internal control over financial reporting and for its assessment of the effectiveness of internal control over financial reporting. Our responsibility is to express an opinion on management's assessment and an opinion on the effectiveness of the company's internal control over financial reporting based on our audit.

We conducted our audit in accordance with the standards of the Public Company Accounting Oversight Board (United States). Those standards require that we plan and perform the audit to obtain reasonable assurance about whether effective internal control over financial reporting was maintained in all material respects. Our audit included obtaining an understanding of internal control over financial reporting, evaluating management's assessment, testing and evaluating the design and operating effectiveness of internal control, and performing such other procedures as we considered necessary in the circumstances. We believe that our audit provides a reasonable basis for our opinion.

A company's internal control over financial reporting is a process designed to provide reasonable assurance regarding the reliability of financial reporting and the preparation of financial statements for external purposes in accordance with generally accepted accounting principles. A company's internal control over financial reporting includes those policies and procedures that (1) pertain to the maintenance of records that, in reasonable detail, accurately and fairly reflect the transactions and dispositions of the assets of the company; (2) provide reasonable assurance that transactions are recorded as necessary to permit preparation of financial statements in accordance with generally accepted accounting principles, and that receipts and expenditures of the company are being made only in accordance with authorizations of management and directors of the company; and (3) provide reasonable assurance regarding prevention or timely detection of unauthorized acquisition, use, or disposition of the company's assets that could have a material effect on the financial statements.

Because of its inherent limitations, internal control over financial reporting may not prevent or detect misstatements. Also, projections of any evaluation of effectiveness to future periods are subject to the risk that controls may become inadequate because of changes in conditions, or that the degree of compliance with the policies or procedures may deteriorate.

In our opinion, management's assessment that Peach Blossom Cologne Company maintained effective internal control over financial reporting as of December 31, 2008, is fairly stated, in all material respects, based on the COSO criteria. Also in our opinion, Peach Blossom Cologne Company maintained, in all material respects, effective internal control over financial reporting as of December 31, 2008, based on the COSO criteria.

We have also audited, in accordance with the standards of the Public Company Accounting Oversight Board (United States), the balance sheets of Peach Blossom Cologne Company as of December 31, 2008 and 2007, and the related statements of income, changes in shareholders' equity, and cash flows for the years then ended, and our report dated February 9, 2009 expressed an unqualified opinion thereon.

Anderson, Olds, and Watershed

Certified Public Accountants
February 9, 2009

Peach Blossom Cologne Company
Management's Report on Internal
Control Over Financial Reporting
December 31, 2008

1308 Bee Hive Boulevard Chicago, Illinois 60615
Phone: 312-477-7288
Fax: 312-477-9999
Internet: www.peachblossom.com

February 5, 2009

Anderson, Olds and Watershed
Certified Public Accountants
615 Big City National Bank Building
Main at Michigan
Chicago, Illinois 60612

Our management is responsible for establishing and maintaining adequate internal control over financial reporting. Under the supervision and with the participation of our management, including our principal executive officer and principal financial officer, we conducted an evaluation of the effectiveness of our internal control over financial reporting based on the framework in *Internal Control–Integrated Framework* issued by the Committee of Sponsoring Organizations of the Treadway Commission (the COSO criteria). Based on our evaluation under the COSO criteria, our management concluded that our internal control over financial reporting was effective as of December 31, 2008. Our management's assessment of the effectiveness of our internal control over financial reporting as of December 31, 2008 has been audited by Anderson, Olds and Watershed, an independent registered public accounting firm, as stated in their report which is included herein.

Lawrence Lancaster
President
Peach Blossom Cologne Company

Parker Shelton
Controller
Peach Blossom Cologne Company

PEACH BLOSSOM COLOGNE COMPANY
Balance Sheet
December 31, 2008 and 2007

ASSETS

	2008	2007
Current Assets:		
Cash	$339,415	$141,692
Accounts receivable less allowance for losses		
2008, $10,485; 2007, $12,250	113,536	115,875
Inventories (Note 1)	777,152	523,255
Total Current Assets	$1,230,103	$780,822
Property, plant, & equipment, at cost (Note 1):		
Land	82,250	103,250
Buildings	276,263	243,250
Machinery and equipment	540,845	535,800
Automotive equipment	99,425	90,125
Office furniture and fixtures	106,433	99,775
	$1,105,216	$1,072,200
Less accumulated depreciation	316,661	252,239
	788,555	819,961
TOTAL ASSETS	$2,018,658	$1,600,783

LIABILITIES AND STOCKHOLDERS' EQUITY

	2008	2007
Current Liabilities:		
Accounts payable	$223,161	$114,113
Accrued interest	10,625	
Notes payable (Note 2)	125,000	
Dividends payable	15,725	12,500
Income taxes payable (Note 3)	23,023	23,336
Total current liabilities	$397,534	$149,949
Total Liabilities	$397,534	$149,949
Stockholders' Equity:		
Common stock, par value $100, authorized 20,000 shares,		
issued and outstanding 9,250 shares	925,000	925,000
Contributed capital in excess of par value	95,979	95,979
Retained earnings	600,145	429,855
Total Stockholders' Equity	$1,621,124	$1,450,834
TOTAL LIABILITIES AND STOCKHOLDERS' EQUITY	$2,018,658	$1,600,783

PEACH BLOSSOM COLOGNE COMPANY
Statement of Income
Years Ended December 31, 2008 and 2007

	2008	2007
Net sales and other revenues	$3,420,942	$3,015,506
Cost of goods sold	1,420,933	1,203,106
Gross margin	2,000,009	1,812,400
Operating expenses:		
Selling, general, and administrative	1,662,687	1,513,625
Depreciation (Note 1)	64,422	60,778
	1,727,109	1,574,403
Operating Income	272,900	237,997
Other income (expense) and adjustments:		
Interest	(27,500)	(22,500)
Gain on sale of fixed assets	18,638	12,360
Net income before federal income taxes	264,038	227,857
Provision for income taxes (Notes 1 and 3)	78,023	65,721
NET INCOME	$186,015	$162,136
Earnings per common share (Note 4)	$20.11	$17.53

PEACH BLOSSOM COLOGNE COMPANY
Statement of Changes in Stockholders' Equity
Years Ended December 31, 2008 and 2007

	2008	2007
Common Stock:		
Common stock at beginning of year	$925,000	$925,000
Common stock at end of year	$925,000	$925,000
Contributed capital:		
Contributed capital at beginning of year	$95,979	$95,979
Contributed capital at end of year	$95,979	$95,979
Retained Earnings:		
Retained earnings at beginning of year	$429,855	$280,219
Net income for the year	186,015	162,136
Dividends	(15,725)	(12,500)
Retained earnings at end of year	$600,145	$429,855

PEACH BLOSSOM COLOGNE COMPANY
Statement of Cash Flows
Years Ended December 31, 2008 and 2007

	2008	2007
Cash flows from operating activities:		
Net income	$186,015	$162,136
Add \<Deduct\> items not using \<providing\> cash:		
Depreciation..	64,422	60,778
Change in accounts receivable...............................	4,104	(3,981)
Change in allowance for bad debts..........................	(1,765)	(5,693)
Change in inventory..	(253,897)	(152,480)
Change in accounts payable....................................	109,048	(20,263)
Change in accrued liabilities...................................	10,625	(14,995)
Change in income taxes payable.............................	(313)	(4,214)
Gain or loss--sale of assets....................................	(18,638)	(12,360)
Net cash provided--operating activities...................	$99,601	$8,928
Cash flows from investing activities:		
Cash provided		
Sale of assets..	39,638	49,600
Cash disbursed		
Purchase of assets..	54,016	74,900
Net cash provided \<used\>--investing activities..............	($14,378)	($25,300)
Cash flows from financing activities:		
Cash provided		
Issuance of notes payable..............................	245,000	120,000
Cash disbursed		
Dividends paid...	12,500	12,500
Payments on notes..	120,000	120,000
Net cash provided \<used\>--financing activities..............	$112,500	($12,500)
Net increase \<decrease\> in cash................................	197,723	(28,872)
Cash at beginning of year..	141,692	170,564
Cash at end of year...	$339,415	$141,692

Supplemental Disclosures of Cash Flow Information

	2008	2007
Interest paid..	$16,875	$14,995
Income taxes paid...	78,336	68,280

PEACH BLOSSOM COLOGNE COMPANY
Notes to Financial Statements
Years Ended December 31, 2008 and 2007

Note 1--Summary of Significant Accounting Policies

The accounting policies employed by the Peach Blossom Cologne Company are in accordance with generally accepted accounting principles. In those instances where more than one generally accepted accounting principle can be applied, the company has adopted the one it believes most accurately and fairly reflects the situation, as described in the following paragraphs.

Inventories--Inventories are stated at the lower-of-cost-or-market. Cost is determined by the first-in, first-out method. Market value is considered to be the current sales price less distribution cost for finished products and replacement cost for other inventories. Physical inventories are taken each year at year-end.

Property, plant, and equipment--Fixed assets are stated at cost. Repair and maintenance, rearrangement costs, and renewals and betterments which do not increase the basic productive capacity of the assets are charged to cost and expensed as incurred. When fixed assets are disposed of, the cost and related accumulated depreciation are removed from the accounts and any resulting gain or loss is reflected in income. Depreciation is provided on groups of assets in the year of acquisition and disposal using the straight-line method.

Definition of accounting year--The accounts of Peach Blossom Cologne Company are on a calendar year basis.

Income taxes--When timing differences between financial and tax reporting occur, deferred income taxes are provided.

Note 2--Long-term and Short-term Debt

Debt outstanding at December 31, 2008, consisted of a $125,000 note to Big City National Bank dated April 30, 2008, due April 30, 2009, unsecured, 12 3/4% interest payable April 30, 2009. There was no debt outstanding at December 31, 2007.

Note 3--Income Taxes

Income Taxes were calculated on 2008 before-tax income of $264,038 and 2007 before-tax net income of $227,857. Applicable tax amounts were $78,023 for 2008 and $65,721 for 2007. Income taxes payable at December 31, 2008 and 2007 were $23,023 and $23,336, respectively.

Note 4--Earnings Per Share

Primary earnings per share are computed by dividing net income by the weighted average number of shares of common stock outstanding during each year. There were no common stock equivalents. Therefore, fully diluted earnings per share are the same as primary earnings per share.

Peach Blossom Cologne Company
Working Trial Balance-Balance Sheet
12-31-08

TB-BS
2-4-09
JWP

		Working Paper Reference	Per Audit 12-31-07	Per Books 12-31-08	Adjustments Debit	Adjustments Credit		Per Audit 12-31-08	Reclassification Items Debit	Reclassification Items Credit	Financial Statements 12-31-08
Assets:											
101	Cash-Big City National Bank	A-1	141,692	339,415				339,415			339,415
105	Accounts receivable	B-1	128,125	124,861		840	(1)	124,021			113,536
106	Allowance for bad debts	B-5	(12,250)	(11,325)	840		(1)	(10,485)			
109	Inventory	C-1	523,255	779,802		2,650	(2)	777,152			777,152
210	Land	D-1	103,250	82,250				82,250			82,250
220	Buildings	D-1	243,250	276,263				276,263			276,263
221	Accum. depn.- buildings	D-1	(56,758)	(65,416)				(65,416)			
230	Machinery and equipment	D-1	535,800	540,845				540,845			540,845
231	Accum. depn.- mach.& equip.	D-1	(133,950)	(160,866)				(160,866)			
240	Automotive equipment	D-1	90,125	99,425				99,425			99,425
241	Accum. depn.- auto. equip.	D-1	(29,105)	(52,798)				(52,798)			
250	Office furniture & fixtures	D-1	99,775	106,433				106,433			106,433
251	Accum. depn.- off. furn.& fix.	D-1	(32,426)	(37,581)				(37,581)	Total acc. depn.		(316,661)
	Total assets		1,600,783	2,021,308				2,018,658			2,018,658
Liabilities:											
301	Accounts payable	E-1	114,113	221,136		2,025	(3)	223,161			223,161
305	Accrued interest	F-1	-	10,625				10,625			10,625
306	Dividends payable		12,500	15,725				15,725			15,725
307	Federal income tax payable	G-1	23,336	20,000		3,023	(4)	23,023			23,023
308	Notes payable-short term	F-1	-	125,000				125,000			125,000
	Total liabilities		149,949	392,486				397,534			397,534
Owners' Equity:											
501	Common stock		925,000	925,000				925,000			925,000
505	Other contributed capital		95,979	95,979				95,979			95,979
601	Retained earnings	H-1	280,219	429,855				429,855			600,145
605	Dividends	H-1	(12,500)	(15,725)				(15,725)			
610	Current net income	TB-IS	162,136	193,713	7,698	-		186,015			
	Total owners' equity		1,450,834	1,628,822				1,621,124			1,621,124
	Total liabilities & owners' equity		1,600,783	2,021,308	8,538	8,538		2,018,658			2,018,658

Peach Blossom Cologne Company
Working Trial Balance-Income Statement
12-31-08

TB-IS
2-4-09
JWP

		Working Paper Reference	Per Audit 12-31-07	Per Books 12-31-08	Adjustments Debit	Adjustments Credit	Per Audit 12-31-08	Reclassification Items Debit	Reclassification Items Credit	Financial Statements 12-31-08
REVENUE:										
701	Sales		3,064,520	3,447,472			3,447,472			3,447,472
703	Sales Returns & Allowances		(49,014)	(26,530)			(26,530)			(26,530)
	Net Sales		3,015,506	3,420,942			3,420,942			3,420,942
EXPENSES:										
801	Cost of Goods Sold		1,203,106	1,418,283	2,650 (2)		1,420,933			1,420,933
	Gross Margin		1,812,400	2,002,659			2,000,009			2,000,009
OPERATING EXPENSES:										
820	Wage and Salary Expense		1,276,848	1,418,720			1,418,720			1,418,720
821	Payroll Tax Expense		89,380	99,310			99,310			99,310
822	Depreciation Expense	D-4	60,778	64,422			64,422			64,422
823	Rent Expense		3,750	3,750			3,750			3,750
824	Office Supplies Expense		7,305	8,615			8,615			8,615
825	Small Tools Expense		2,362	2,988			2,988			2,988
826	Advertising Expense		6,630	6,313			6,313			6,313
827	Insurance		12,925	15,737			15,737			15,737
828	Repairs and Maintenance	D-5	12,024	17,869			17,869			17,869
829	Property Tax		14,793	13,463			13,463			13,463
830	Utilities		10,252	8,645	2,025 (3)		10,670			10,670
831	Professional Fees		27,250	26,875			26,875			26,875
832	Miscellaneous Expense		6,114	302			302			302
833	Provision for Bad Debts	B-5	10,250	9,925			9,925			9,925
834	Freight Expense		33,742	28,150			28,150			28,150
	Total Operating Expenses		1,574,403	1,725,084			1,727,109			1,727,109
	Net Income From Operations		237,997	277,575			272,900			272,900
OTHER INCOME (EXPENSE):										
901	Interest Expense	F-1	(22,500)	(27,500)			(27,500)			(27,500)
930	Gain(Loss)Sale of Fixed Assets	D-3	12,360	18,638			18,638			18,638
950	Miscellaneous Income		-	-			-			-
	Net Other Income		(10,140)	(8,862)			(8,862)			(8,862)
	Net Income Before Taxes		227,857	268,713			264,038			264,038
940	Federal Income Tax	G-1	65,721	75,000	3,023 (4)		78,023			78,023
	Net Income		162,136	193,713	7,698		186,015			186,015

161

Peach Blossom Cologne Company		AJE		
Proposed Adjusting Journal Entries		2-4-09		
December 31, 2008		JWP		

Account Description		Account Number	Debit	Credit
(AJE # 1)				
Allowance for bad debts		106	840	
Accounts receivable		105		840
To write off uncollectible				
accounts per (B-1).				
(AJE # 2)				
Cost of goods sold		801	2650	
Inventory		109		2650
To correct inventory extension				
error per (C-1).				
(AJE # 3)				
Utilities expense		830	2025	
Accounts payable		301		2025
To record unrecorded liability				
per (E-1).				
(AJE # 4)				
Federal income tax expense		940	3023	
Federal income taxes payable		307		3023
To adjust federal income taxes				
per (G-1).				

	Peach Blossom Cologne Company	RJE		
	Proposed Reclassifying Journal Entries	2-4-09		
	December 31, 2008	JWP		

	Account Description	Account Number	Debit	Credit
	None required			

ANDERSON, OLDS, & WATERSHED

Certified Public Accountants
615 Big City National Bank Building
Main at Michigan Avenue
Chicago, Illinois 60612
Phone: (312) 555-4452
Fax: (312) 555-9991
Internet: www.aowcpa.com

February 5, 2009

To Management and the Audit Committee of the Board of Directors, Peach Blossom Cologne Company:

We have completed our audit of internal control over financial reporting performed in conjunction with our audit of the financial statements of Peach Blossom Cologne Company for the year ended December 31, 2008. PCAOB Auditing Standard 2 requires that we provide a written communication to management and the Audit Committee of the Board of Directors of all significant deficiencies and material weaknesses that we discovered during that audit. In addition, we are required to report to management, in writing, all deficiencies in internal control over financial reporting.

The following definitions from Auditing Standard 2 are applicable:

Internal Control Deficiency – An internal control deficiency exists when the design or operation of a control does not allow management or employees, in the normal course of performing their assigned functions, to prevent or detect misstatements on a timely basis.

Significant Deficiency – A control deficiency, or combination of control deficiencies, that adversely affects the company's ability to initiate, authorize, record, process, or report external financial data reliably in accordance with generally accepted accounting principles such that there is more than a remote likelihood that a misstatement of the company's annual or interim financial statements, that is more than inconsequential, will not be prevented or detected.

Material Weakness – A significant deficiency, or combination of significant deficiencies, that results in more than a remote likelihood that a material misstatement of the annual or interim financial statements will not be prevented or detected.

We found no material weaknesses. We did uncover the following significant deficiency. This item should be corrected within a reasonable period of time:

- Cash receipts are not deposited intact daily. As a consequence, the possibility exists that an employee could misappropriate, or lose, cash receipts. We recommend that all cash receipts be deposited intact on a daily basis.

We also discovered the following internal control deficiency:

- Not all personnel with financial responsibilities are required to take annual vacations. This situation could lead to someone perpetrating a fraud and being in a position to cover up that fraud for a significant period of time. We recommend that all such persons be required to take annual vacations.

This report is intended solely for the use of the Board of Directors, management, and others within the organization. If you would like to discuss any of these matters, we would be pleased to review them with you.

Very truly yours,

Anderson, Olds, and Watershed

Anderson, Olds, and Watershed
Certified Public Accountants

Peach Blossom Cologne Company						A-1	
Bank Reconciliation-Big City National Bank						1-21-09	
12-31-08						JWP	
Prepared by Client							

Balance Per Bank Statement						447690	C#
Add:							
Deposit in Transit		Dec 31				16970	u
Deduct:						464660	
Checks outstanding							
No.	Payee						
1063	Fruit Juicy Perfume Co.		Dec. 29		12268N		
1064	Norton Exterminators		Dec. 29		2790N		
1065	Petrozine Fuel Co.		Dec. 29		7300N		
1073	Fruit Scents, Inc.		Dec. 30		5895N		
1075	Fruit Juicy Perfume Co.		Dec. 30		11250N		
1076	Flash Freight Co.		Dec. 30		3000N		
1077	Fruit Juicy Perfume Co.		Dec. 30		32000N		
1080	Longhorn Garbage Disposal		Dec. 30		45N		
1081	Fruit Scents, Inc.		Dec. 31		8250N		
1082	Flash Freight Co.		Dec. 31		4017N		
1083	National Trucks		Dec. 31		805N		
1084	United Parcel Co.		Dec. 31		125N		
1085	Fruit Scents, Inc.		Dec. 31		37500N		
						125245	
	Balance Per Books 12-31-08					339415	
						^	
Audit adjustments:						(TB-BS)	
None required							
Balance per audit						339415	
^	Footed						
#	Agreed to beginning balance of cutoff bank statement.						
C	Confirmed with bank per (A-2).						
u	Traced to cash receipts journal entry before year-end and to cutoff bank statment.						
N	Examined paid checks clearing with cutoff bank statement and traced to cash disbursements						
	journal for Dec. 2008.						

STANDARD FORM TO CONFIRM ACCOUNT
BALANCE INFORMATION WITH FINANCIAL INSTITUTIONS

ORIGINAL
To be mailed to accountant

Peach Blossom Cologne Co.

CUSTOMER NAME

Financial Institution's Name and Address

[Big City National Bank
Big City National Bank Building
Main at Michigan Avenue
[Chicago, Illinois 60612   ]

We have provided to our accountants the following information as of the close of business on **December 31, xx 2008** regarding our deposit and loan balances. Please confirm the accuracy of the information, noting any exceptions to the information provided. If the balances have been left blank, please complete this form by furnishing the balance in the appropriate space below.* Although we do not request nor expect you to conduct a comprehensive, detailed search of your records, if during the process of completing this confirmation additional information about other deposit and loan accounts we may have with you comes to your attention, please include such information below. Please use the enclosed envelope to return the form directly to our accountants.

1. At the close of business on the date listed above, our records indicated the following deposit balance(s):

ACCOUNT NAME	ACCOUNT NO.	INTEREST RATE	BALANCE*
Peach Blossom Cologne Company	58-4329	N/A	$447,690 *A-1*

2. We were directly liable to the financial institution for loans at the close of business on the date listed above as follows:

ACCOUNT NO./ DESCRIPTION	BALANCE*	DATE DUE	INTEREST RATE	DATE THROUGH WHICH INTEREST IS PAID	DESCRIPTION OF COLLATERAL
A/C # 013756	$125,000 F-1	4-30-09	12-3/4%	Int. is paid through 4/30/08	Unsecured

Lillian Stockton
(Customer's Authorized Signature)

January 2, 2009
(Date)

The information presented above by the customer is in agreement with our records. Although we have not conducted a comprehensive, detailed search of our records, no other deposit or loan accounts have come to our attention except as noted below.

Buford Churchill
(Financial Institution Authorized Signature)

Cashier
(Title)

January 7, 2009
(Date)

EXCEPTIONS AND/OR COMMENTS

Please return this form directly to our accountants:

[Anderson, Olds, and Watershed
615 Big City National Bank Bldg.
Main at Michigan Avenue
Chicago, Illinois 60612
[   ]

* Ordinarily, balances are intentionally left blank if they are not available at the time the form is prepared.

Approved 1990 by American Bankers Association, American Institute of Certified Public Accountants, and Bank Administration Institute. Additional forms available from: AICPA – Order Department, P.O. Box 1003, NY, NY 10108-1003

D451 5851

Peach Blossom Cologne Company
Accounts Receivable - Aged Trial Balance
12-31-08
(Prepared by Client)

B-1
1-23-09
JWP

Customer	Current 1-30 days	30-60 Days	60-90 Days	Over 90 Days	Total		Confirm Mailed 1-2-09	Subsequent Collection to 1-14-09	Comments by Credit Manager--B. Robertson
All-Right Discount Drugs		2382@			2382@		negative	---	Sometimes slow. Good account.
Bobell Beauty Supplies			4943@		4943@		negative	---	Slow paying.
Body Bar	2500@	500@	645@		3645@		negative	2645R	Slow paying, but always does.
Cut-Rate Discount Stores	1450@	1050@	250@		2750@		negative	1250R	Slow paying. Good account.
Darings	2125@				2125@		negative	1900R	
Frankies Floral Frag.	5500@	5000@			10500@	C(B-2)	positive	---	Good Account.
Kanine Kaffeurs				840@	840@	#(B-3)	positive	---	Company out of business.
Lone Star Supply	2002@				2002@		negative	1500R	
Rausch's Dept.Store	2250@	875@			3125@		negative	2125R	Good Account.
Tears and Doefall Co.	44800@	6200@	5250@		56250@	C(B-3)	positive	43000R	Sometimes slow--good account.
William's Fragrances	9700@	2050@			11750@	C(B-4)	positive	9000R	Good Account.
Young and Beautiful	11250@				11250@	C(B-4)	positive	11250R	
Various Other Acct's.	10299@		3000@		13299@			---	Some slow, but all good accounts.
Per client	91876	18057	14088	840	124861			72670	
	<	<	<	<	^^				
Audit adjustments									Percentage of accounts receivable collected
(AJE #1)				(840)	(840)	(TB-BS)			as of 1/14/09:
Per audit	91876	18057	14088	-	124021			$72,670/12	59%

< Footed.
^^ Footed and crossfooted.
@ Balances and aging traced from subsidiary ledger. No exceptions noted.
C Positive confirmation mailed. No exceptions noted.
Confirmation sent; returned by post office unopened. Propose (AJE #1) to write off receivable:

106 Allowance for bad debts	840		
105 Accounts receivable		840	

R Corresponds with entry in cash receipts journal.
Note: No negative confirmations were returned.

January 2, 2009

Frankie's Floral Fragrances
602 River Street
Chicago, Illinois 60617

Dear Sir or Madam:

For the purpose of providing independent confirmation of our accounts receivable, please advise our auditors, Anderson, Olds, and Watershed, Certified Public Accountants, of the correctness of your balance with us as of December 31, 2008, as shown on the enclosed statement.

After comparing the statement with your records, please sign the confirmation below and return it directly to our auditors in the enclosed, addressed envelope. If your records differ from the balance shown, please note your **exceptions** below.

This letter is *not* a request for payment, but merely for confirmation of your account balance.

Very truly yours,
PEACH BLOSSOM COLOGNE COMPANY
By_____*Parker Shelton*_____

CONFIRMATION OF ACCOUNTS RECEIVABLE

Confirmation Request No. __1__

Anderson, Olds, and Watershed
Certified Public Accountants
615 Big City National Bank Building
Main at Michigan Avenue
Chicago, Illinois 60612

Dear Sir or Madam:

The statement of our account showing a balance of $____10,500____ as of ____12/31/08____ is correct except as noted below.   *(B-1)*

Very truly yours,
Frankie,s Floral Fragrances
James Whitmore
Chief Accountant

Date   January 16, 2009

Exceptions:
            No exceptions

_____

Peach Blossom Cologne Company   **B-3**
Receivables Confirmation   *1-22-09*
December 31, 2008   *JWP*

CONFIRMATION OF ACCOUNTS RECEIVABLE

Confirmation Request No. __2__

Anderson, Olds, and Watershed
Certified Public Accountants
615 Big City National Bank Building
Main at Michigan Avenue
Chicago, Illinois 60612

Dear Sir or Madam:

The statement of our account showing a balance of $___840___ as of ___12/31/08___ is correct except as noted below.   *(B-1)*

Very truly yours,

Date _____

_____

_____

Exceptions:

Confirmation from Kanine Kaffeurs returned by post office unopened. Should write off as bad debt.
Reference (B-1) for proposed AJE. JWP

CONFIRMATION OF ACCOUNTS RECEIVABLE

Confirmation Request No. __3__

Anderson, Olds, and Watershed
Certified Public Accountants
615 Big City National Bank Building
Main at Michigan Avenue
Chicago, Illinois 60612

Dear Sir or Madam:

(1)

The statement of our account showing a balance of $__56,250__ as of ___12/31/08___ is correct except as noted below.   *(B-1)*

Very truly yours,
Tears and Doefall Company

Date   January 19, 2009   *William Okeefe*

                              Controller

Exceptions:

None.   *(1) Traced $43,000 of this amount to January collection recorded in cash receipts journal per*

(B-1).JWP

CONFIRMATION OF ACCOUNTS RECEIVABLE

Confirmation Request No. __4__

Anderson, Olds, and Watershed
Certified Public Accountants
615 Big City National Bank Building
Main at Michigan Avenue
Chicago, Illinois 60612

Dear Sir or Madam:

(1)

The statement of our account showing a balance of \$__11,750__ as of __12/31/08__ is correct except as
noted below.   (B-1)

Very truly yours,
William's Fragrances _____

Date __January 20, 2009__   *William Brown* _____
Exceptions:
__No exceptions.__

(1) Traced \$9,000 of this amount to January collection recorded in cash receipts journal per (B-1). JWP

CONFIRMATION OF ACCOUNTS RECEIVABLE
Confirmation Request No. __5__

Anderson, Olds, and Watershed
Certified Public Accountants
615 Big City National Bank Building
Main at Michigan Avenue
Chicago, Illinois 60612

Dear Sir or Madam:

(1)

The statement of our account showing a balance of \$__11,250__ as of __12/31/08__ is correct except as
noted below.   *(B-1)*

Very truly yours,
Young and Beautiful _____

Date __January 16, 2009__   *Roger McAdams* _____
                                                      President

Exceptions:
None.

(1) Traced \$11,250 to January collection recorded in cash receipts journal per (B-1) JWP.

				Allowance for Bad Debts		Provision for Bad Debts	
Peach Blossom Cologne Company						**B-5**	
Allowance for Bad Debts						**1-23-09**	
12-31-08						**JWP**	

				Allowance for Bad Debts		Provision for Bad Debts	
Balance at 12-31-07				12250	A		
	2008 write-offs			10850	Y		
				1400			
	2008 provision			9925	Z	9925	
Balance per client at 12-31-08				11325		9925	
				(TB-BS)		(TB-IS)	
Adjusting journal entries:							
	(AJE # 1) (B-1)			(840)			
Adjusted balance				10485	(2) N	9925	
Journal entry to adjust allowance account:							
(None required - not considered material)							
Balance per audit				10485		9925	
		Provision For Bad Debts Reasonableness Test:					
					EXPECTED		
			AGED		UNCOLL.	EST	
		AGE	AMOUNT		PERCENT	UNCOLL.	
		1-30	91876	(B-1)	1.50%	1378	
		30-60	18057	(B-1)	10.00%	1806	
		60-90	14088	(B-1)	50.00%	7044	
		Over 90	0	(1)	100.00%	0	
		Balance per Analysis				10228	
		Adjusted Balance				10485	(2) N
		Difference				257	
A	Agreed to prior year's working papers.						
Y	All write-offs approved by credit manager.						
Z	Provision appears reasonable and in line						
	with prior years.						
N	Allowance balance per reasonableness test is lower than client balance						
	per books. Client declined to reduce the account. The adjusted balance						
	appears reasonable and is in line with prior year. As the adjustment						
	would increase income and is less than 1% of net income (before						
	adjustments), no adjustment is considered necessary. JWP						
(1) $840 - $840 = 0							
(B-1) (AJE #1)							

Peach Blossom Cologne Company
Inventory
12-31-08

Item	Size (Ounces)	Number of Cases	Number of Bottles (24/Case)	Total Ounces	Cost per Unit	Amount Inventory	Totals
Oils							
#A601 Lemon	2	372.00	8928	17856N	2.50/oz<	44640Y	
#A603 Lemon	4	146.00	3504	14016N	2.50/oz<	35040Y	
#A608 Lemon	6	104.00	2496	14976N	2.50/oz<	37440Y	
#R315 Apple	4	114.00	2736	10944N	2.25/oz<	24624Y	
#R320 Apple	6	25.00	600	3600N	2.25/oz<	8100Y	
#Q291 Magnolia	8	31.00	744	5952N	2.11/oz<	12559Y	
Total Oils:							162403
Cremes							
#H84 Hand Creme	4	613.33	14720N	---	4.00/btl<	58880Y	
#F60 Face Creme	4	580.00	13920N	---	4.25/btl<	59160Y	
Total Cremes							118040
Lotions							
#L612 Moisturizing	8	740.00	17760N	---	3.00/btl<	53280Y	
#L940 Skin Tone	8	758.00	18192N	---	2.86/btl<	54679K	
#L818 Smoothing	8	784.00	18816N	---	2.73/btl<	51368Y	
Total Lotions							159327
Colognes							
#E801 L'Eau de Pomme	8	190.00	4560	36480N	2.80/oz<	102144Y	
#E802 L'Eau de Abricot	8	97.50	2340	18720N	2.80/oz<	52416Y	
#E803 L'Eau de Teint	8	80.00	1920	15360N	2.80/oz<	43008Y	
#E804 L'Eau de Chevrefeuille	8	50.00	1200	9600N	2.80/oz<	26880Y	
#E805 L'Eau de Jasmin	8	42.50	1020	8160N	2.80/oz<	22848Y	
#E806 L'Eau de Citron	8	62.50	1500	12000N	2.80/oz<	33600Y	
#E807 L'Eau de Rose	8	110.00	2640	21120N	2.80/oz<	59136Y	
Total Colognes							340032
Per client 12-31-02		4899.83<	117596<	---	---	------	779802
							<
				Audit adjustments:			(TB-BS)
				(AJE # 2)			(2650)
				Per audit			777152

Note:
Current cost obtained and found to exceed inventory carrying value. No lower of cost or market adjustment necessary. JWP

^ Footed
Y Extensions recalculated.
N Quantities traced from inventory observation.
< FIFO costing vouched to vendor invoice (freight and discounts included where applicable.)
K Client error in extending--should be $52,029. Propose (AJE #3) to correct:
801 Cost of goods sold   2650
109 Inventory   2650

	Peach Blossom Cologne Company			C-2			
	Inventory Observation and Test Counts			1-1-09			
	December 31, 2008			JWP			

Stock Num- ber	Item	Number of Cases	Number of Bottles (24/Case)	Size of Bottle	Total Ounces			
STOREROOM:			C					
L818	Smoothing Lotion	704n	16896*	8 oz	135168			
L612	Moisturizing Lotion	740	17760*	8 oz	142080			
L940	Skin Tone Lotion	758n	18192*	8 oz	145536			
F60	Face Creme	580	13920*	4 oz	55680			
H84	Hand Creme	493 1/3n	11840*	4 oz	47360			
E804	L'Eau de Chevrefeuille	50n	1200	8 oz	9600*			
E806	L'Eau de Citron Cologne	42 1/2n	1020	8 oz	8160*			
E805	L'Eau de Jasmin Cologne	42 1/2n	1020	8 oz	8160*			
E807	L'Eau de Rose Cologne	70n	1680	8 oz	13440*			
E801	L'Eau de Pomme Cologne	160	3840	8 oz	30720*			
E802	L'Eau d'Abricot Cologne	97 1/2	2340	8 oz	18720*			
E803	L'Eau de Teint Cologne	80	1920	8 oz	15360*			
R320	Apple Oil	25n	600	6 oz	3600*			
Q291	Magnolia Oil	21n	504	8 oz	4032*			
R315	Apple Oil	114	2736	4 oz	10944*			
A608	Lemon Oil	104	2496	6 oz	14976*			
A603	Lemon Oil	106n	2544	4 oz	10176*			
A601	Lemon Oil	372	8928	2 oz	17856*			
	Storeroom Total	4559 5/6	109436		691568			
SHIPPING DOCK:								
E806	L'Eau de Citron Cologne	20n	480	8 oz	3840*			
E807	L'Eau de Rose Cologne	40n	960	8 oz	7680*			
H84	Hand Creme	120	2880*	4 oz	11520			
Q291	Magnolia Oil	10n	240	8 oz	1920*			
E801	L'Eau de Pomme Cologne	30n	720	8 oz	5760*			
L818	Smoothing Lotion	80	1920*	8 oz	15360			
A603	Lemon Oil	40	960	4 oz	3840*			
	Shipping Dock Total	340	8160		49920			
	Total Inventory	4899 5/6	117596		741488			

C	After testing 30 unopened cases, bottle count on vendor's label accepted on unopened cases.						
n	Test counted during observation. No errors observed.						
NOTE:	No obsolete or damaged inventory was observed.						
NOTE:	For cutoff last receiving report #12-05 was used on 12/30/08. 114 3/4 cases of #A601 Lemon Oil						
	were received from Fruit Scents, Inc. That shipment included in above inventory. (On 1/21/09, traced						
	this shipment to voucher #12-29. JWP)						
*	On 1/21/09: traced these quantities into client's final priced inventory on working paper (C-1) JWP.						

Peach Blossom Cologne Company
Inventory Observation Memo
December 31, 2008

I arrived at the client's plant at 1308 Bee Hive Boulevard, Chicago, Illinois, at 8:00 AM on January 1, 2009, to observe the client's physical inventory. The plant was closed this day for the inventory counting. I reviewed the client's inventory instructions, which appeared adequate. I then observed the client personnel as they took a 100% inventory. I recorded test counts on (C-2) for later tracing to the client's final priced inventory.

The client's housekeeping was good and the inventory neat and orderly to facilitate an accurate count. The client's plant is divided into two inventory areas: the main storeroom and the shipping dock. All inventory is received from vendors in 24-bottle cases.

In my opinion, the client used good inventory procedures and took an accurate count. The client's inventory personnel seemed competent, and good control was exercised throughout the inventory procedures. Since the plant was shut down, inventory cutoff was not a problem. The last shipment of inventory was received on 12/30/08 from Fruit Scents Inc. (114 3/4 cases of #A601 Lemon Oil) and is included in the inventory count. I did not observe any obsolete or damaged inventory.

Jasper W. Parsons
Audit Senior
1-1-09

Peach Blossom Cologne Company
Property, Plant and Equipment
12-31-08
(Prepared by Client)

D-1
1-27-09
JWP

Asset Description	Asset Cost				Depreciation Rate-Method	Accumulated Deprec.			
	Beg. Bal.	Additions	Disposals	End. Bal.		Beg. Bal.	Expense Additions	Disposals	End. Bal.
Land	103250 Z	-0- (D-2)	21000 (D-3)	82250 (TB-BS)	---	---	---	---	---
Buildings	243250 Z	33013 (D-2)	---	276263 (TB-BS)	3 1/3% S.L (30 YEARS)	56758 Z	8658 (D-4)	---	65416 (TB-BS)
Machinery & Equipment (Plant)	535800 Z	5045 (D-2)	---	540845 (TB-BS)	5% S.L. (20 YEARS)	133950 Z	26916 (D-4)	---	160866 (TB-BS)
Automotive	90125 Z	9300 (D-2)	---	99425 (TB-BS)	25% S.L. (4 YEARS)	29105 Z	23693 (D-4)	---	52798 (TB-BS)
Office Furniture and Fixtures	99775 Z	6658 (D-2)	--- (D-3)	106433 (TB-BS)	5% S.L. (20 YEARS)	32426 Z	5155 (D-4)	---	37581 (TB-BS)
Per client	1072200	54016	21000	1105216		252239	64422 (TB-IS)	-0-	316661
Audit adjustments:	<	<	<	^^		<		<	^^
Per audit	1072200	54016	21000	1105216		252239	64422	-0-	316661

< Footed.
^^ Crossfooted.
Z Agreed to prior year's audit working papers.

176

Peach Blossom Cologne Company
Additions to Property, Plant, and Equipment
12-31-08

(Prepared by Client)

D-2
1-27-09
JWP

Vo. No.	Vendor	Item Description	Cost
3-26	Taggart Construction, Chicago, IL	Construction of garage & maintenance shop for automobile fleet.	33013 AF@
5-18	Bobbie Butler Ford, Chicago, IL	2005 Focus	9300 AF@
7-20	Hart-Murphy Office Outfitters, Chicago, IL	Four (4) used Delta computers for office with one yr. service contract @ $1095 ea.	4380 AF@
7-21	Hart-Murphy Office Outfitters, Chicago, IL	Eight Kardex filing cabinets at $284.75 ea.	2278 AF@
10-14	Edwards and Johnson Industrial Supply Co. St. Louis, MO	Atwell-Henley box folding machine	5045 AF@
	Per client		54016 (1)
	Audit adjustments:		^ (D-1)
	Per audit		54016

SUMMARY ADDITIONS PER AUDIT ANALYSIS:

Voucher	Buildings	Machinery	Auto	Office	Total
3-26	33013 N				33013
5-18			9300 N		9300
7-20				4380 N	4380
7-21				2278 N	2278
10-14		5045 N			5045
Totals	33013	5045	9300	6658	54016
	< (D-1)	< (D-1)	< (D-1)	< (D-1)	< (1)

N Agree with classification of each asset.
A Vouched to vendor's invoice.
^ Footed.
F Physically observed the asset.
@ Noted approval of addition in minutes of Board of Directors meeting.

Peach Blossom Cologne Company   D-3

Retirements of Property, Plant, and Equipment   1-29-09

12-31-08   JWP

(Prepared by Client)

Journal Vo. No.	Asset Description	Date Acquired	Date Sold	Depreciation Rate-Method	Cost	Accum, Deprec.	Book Value	Proceeds	Gain (Loss) on Disposal
3-12	Vacant lot located at 1212 Westminster Road Chicago, Illinois	2-12-00 @	3-20-08 e	---	21000 @	0	21000 r	39638 y	18638 r
					(D-1)	(D-1)			
	Per client				21000	0	21000	39638	18638
					<	<	<	<	<<
	Audit adjustments:								
									(TB-IS)
	Balance per audit				21000	0	21000	39638	18638

^ Footed.

^^ Crossfooted.

@ Agreed with fixed asset subsidiary ledger.

r Recalculated mathematical operation.

y Traced to cash receipts journal.

e Disposal of fixed asset authorized by Board of Directors per minutes.

	Peach Blossom Cologne Company			D-4	
	Depreciation Computation			1-27-09	
	12-31-08			JWP	
	(Prepared by client)				

Asset	Amount	Rate	2008 Deprec. Provision	Totals
BUILDINGS:				
Held full year #	243250	3.33%	8108 R	
Additions @	33013	1.67%	550 R	
Retirements &	0	1.67%		8658
MACH. & EQUIPMENT:				(D-1)
Held full year #	535800	5.00%	26790 R	
Additions @	5045	2.50%	126 R	
Retirements &	0	2.50%		26916
AUTOMOTIVE :				(D-1)
Held full year #	90125	25.00%	22531 R	
Additions @	9300	12.50%	1162 R	
Retirements &	0	12.50%		23693
OFFICE FURN & FIXTURES:				(D-1)
Held full year #	99775	5.00%	4989 R	
Additions @	6658	2.50%	166 R	
Retirements &	0	2.50%		5155
				(D-1)
Per client			64422	64422
Audit adjustments:			^	^
				(D-1)
Per audit				64422

NOTE:	Assets held for full year computed by deducting				
	retirements from beginning balance.		JWP		
NOTE:	One-half year's depreciation is recorded for all additions and retirements regardless				
	of date of acquisition or disposal.		JWP		
NOTE:	Asset lives appear reasonable, as does depreciation expense.				
NOTE:	Depreciation rates agree with those used in prior year.				
^	Footed.				
R	Recomputed mathematical operation.				
#	Amounts traced to prior year's working papers.				
@	Amounts traced to working paper (D-2).				
&	Amounts traced to working paper (D-3).				

179

	Peach Blossom Cologne Company			D-5	
	Repairs and Maintenance Account			1-28-09	
	12-31-08			JWP	
	(Prepared by client)				

Vo. No.	Vendor	Item Description			Cost
2-18	Smith and Louis Contractors	Repair leaks in the roof of warehouse.			895 u
3-4	Meyer Belt and Conveyor	Repair torn conveyor belt in boxing area.			518 u
5-40	Lone Wolf Painting	Repaint plant offices.			6400 u
10-16	Alex McBane Heat. & Air Cond.	Annual servicing of furnace & heating systems			2686 u
11-28	Texas Metals	Repair and replace handrails on shipping dock.			3358 u
					13857
		Vouchers less than $500 not listed.			4012
		Per client			17869
		Audit adjustments:			^
					(TB-IS)
		Balance per audit			17869
^	Footed				
u	Examined vouchers and supporting documents. Reasonably classified as repairs and maintenance.				

Peach Blossom Cologne Company				E-1
Accounts Payable				1-28-09
12-31-08				JWP
(Prepared by client)				

Vo. No.	Vendor		Amount	
11-18	Fruit Scents, Inc.		89880	uyC (E-3)
12-15	Edwards, Overstreet & Gilley		3600	uy
12-28	Flash Freight Co.		4461	uy
12-29	Fruit Scents, Inc.		14000	uyC (E-3)
12-32	Fruit Juicy Perfume Co.		85875	uyC (E-4)
12-34	Steck Hamilton		2300	uy
12-36	Hammel, Hammel & Johnson		6725	uy
12-37	Fruit Scents, Inc.		14295	uyC (E-3)
	Per client 12-31-08		221136	
			^	
	Audit adjustments:		(TB-BS)	
	(AJE #3) (E-2)		2025	
	Balance per audit		223161	
^	Footed			
u	Traced to cash disbursements journal. Paid after 1-1-09.			
y	Vouched to vendor's invoice and other supporting documents.			
	All items received on or before year-end, 12-31-08.			
C	Confirmed.			

		Peach Blossom Cologne Company				E-2
		Search for Unrecorded Liabilities				1-27-09
		12-31-08				JWP

Vo. No.	Vendor	Invoice Date/ Terms		Comments		Un-recorded Amount
1-14	Central Power & Light	12-26-08		December services		2025 X
						2025
X	Vouched to vendor's invoice and other supporting documents.					
	Represents December service or merchandise. Propose					
	(AJE #3):					
	830 Utilities expense 2025					
	301 Accounts payable 2025					
NOTE:	Reviewed all cash vouchers and supporting documents for period					
	January 1, 2009 to January 9, 2009, as well as unmatched invoice					
	and receiver files for period January 1, 2009 to January 23, 2009.					
	No January vouchers represented merchandise or services on or prior to					
	December 31, 2008, except as noted.					

Peach Blossom Cologne Company
Attorney's Letter
December 31, 2008

A.L./E-5
1 of 2
2-4-09
JWP

Edwards, Overstreet, and Gilley
Attorneys at Law
1604 South Fourth . Chicago, Illinois 60614
Phone: 312-555-3892
Fax: 312-555-9998

January 21, 2009

Anderson, Olds and Watershed
Certified Public Accountants
615 Big City National Bank Building
Main at Michigan Avenue
Chicago, Illinois 60612

Re: Peach Blossom Cologne Company

Dear Sir or Madam:

By letter dated January 2, 2009, Mr. Lawrence Lancaster of Peach Blossom Cologne Company (The "Company") has requested us to furnish you with certain information in connection with your examination of the accounts of the Company as of December 31, 2008. While this firm represents the Company on a regular basis, our engagement has been limited to specific matters as to which we were consulted by the Company.

Subject to the foregoing and to the last paragraph of this letter we advise you that since January 1, 2008 we have not been engaged to give substantive attention to, or represent the Company in connection with material loss contingencies coming within the scope of clause (a) of Paragraph 5 of the Statement of Policy referred to in the last paragraph of this letter.

The information set forth herein is as of the date of this letter and we disclaim any undertaking to advise you of changes which thereafter may be brought to our attention.

This response is limited by, and in accordance with, the ABA Statement of Policy Regarding Lawyers' Responses to Auditors' Requests for Information (December 1975); without limiting the generality of the foregoing, the limitation set forth in such Statement on the scope and use of this response (Paragraphs 2 and 7) are specifically incorporated herein by reference, and any description herein of any "loss contingencies" is qualified in its entirety by Paragraph 5 of the Statement and the accompanying Commentary (which is an integral part of the Statement).

(Continued)

Peach Blossom Cologne Company
Attorney's Letter
December 31, 2008

A.L./E-5
2 of 2
2-4-09
JWP

Page Two

Consistent with the last sentence of Paragraph 6 of the ABA Statement of Policy and pursuant to the Company's request, this will confirm as correct the Company's understanding as set forth in its audit inquiry letter to us that whenever, in the course of performing legal services for the Company with respect to a matter recognized to involve an unasserted possible claim or assessment that may call for financial statement disclosure, we have formed a professional conclusion that the Company must disclose or consider disclosure concerning such possible claim or assessment, we, as a matter of professional responsibility to the Company, will so advise the Company and will consult with the Company concerning the question of such disclosure and the applicable requirements of Statement of Financial Accounting Standards No. 5.

Very truly yours,

EDWARDS, OVERSTREET AND GILLEY

Michael Overstreet
Michael Overstreet
Partner

Peach Blossom Cologne Company
Letter of Representations
December 31, 2008

L.O.R./E-6
1 of 4
2-5-09
JWP

1308 Beehive Boulevard Chicago, Illinois 60615
Phone: 312-477-7288
Fax: 312-477-9999
Internet: www.peachblossom.com

February 5, 2009

Anderson, Olds and Watershed
Certified Public Accountants
615 Big City National Bank Building
Main at Michigan
Chicago, Illinois 60612

The following representations are made to you in connection with your examination of the financial statements of Peach Blossom Cologne Company as of December 31, 2008 for the purpose of expressing an opinion as to whether the financial statements present fairly, in all material respects, the financial position, results of operations, and cash flows of Peach Blossom Cologne Company in conformity with generally accepted accounting principles.

We confirm that we are responsible for the statement of financial position, results of operations, and cash flows in conformity with generally accepted accounting principles. Certain representations in this letter are described as being limited to matters that are material. Items are considered material, regardless of size, if they involve an omission or misstatement of accounting information that, in the light of surrounding circumstances, makes it probable that the judgment of a reasonable person relying on the information would be changed or influenced by the omission or misstatement.

We further confirm that the following representations made to you during your audit examination are accurate to the best of our knowledge and belief:

Financial Statements
The financial statements referred to above are fairly presented in conformity with generally accepted accounting principles. All material transactions have been properly recorded in the accounting records underlying the financial statements. No fraud exists involving management or employees who have significant roles in internal control or others that could have a material effect on the financial statements. No shortages or irregularities have been discovered that have not been disclosed to you, and to our knowledge there is nothing reflecting upon the honesty of members of our organization. The company has no plans that could materially affect the carrying value or classification of assets or liabilities.

Continued

187

Peach Blossom Cologne Company
Letter of Representations
December 31, 2008

L.O.R./E-6
2 of 4
2-5-09
JWP

Page Two

Receivables

Trade Accounts receivable, net, in the amount of $ __113,536__ are valid receivables and do not include any amounts for goods shipped on consignment or approval. In our opinion, the balance in Allowance for Bad Debts of $ __10,485__ is sufficient to cover any losses, discounts, or allowances that may be incurred or allowed in the collection of the receivables.

Inventories:

The Company's inventory in the amount of $ __777,152__ as determined by actual count by competent employees under the supervision of management as of December 31, 2008 are fairly stated on the first-in, first-out, lower-of-cost-or-market basis. Reasonable allowance has been made for slow-moving, obsolete, unsaleable, or unusable items. All inventories are the property of the Company. Inventory balances do not include (1) amounts of goods consigned to the Company, (2) merchandise billed to customers on or before the inventory date, or (3) any items for which the liability has not been provided on the books.

Property, Plant, and Equipment:

Property, plant and equipment is owned with satisfactory title. Capitalizable charges and purchased additions during the year are stated at cost. Property disposed of or abandoned was removed from the accounts. The provision for depreciation in the amount of $ __64,422__ was determined on a basis consistent with preceding years. In our opinion, depreciation methods used and depreciable lives assigned are appropriate for allocating the cost of the assets over their useful lives. The valuation account, accumulated depreciation (balance of __$316,661__), is reasonably adequate to state property, plant, and equipment assets at a reasonable book value with respect to the utilization expected over their remaining lives.

Owned Assets:

The Company had satisfactory title to all owned assets at December 31, 2008. All significant mortgages, assignments, pledges, or other encumbrances of assets have been disclosed to you.

Liabilities:

With the possible exception of a few minor amounts, all direct liabilities of the Company amount to $ __397,534__ and were recorded on the books as of December 31, 2008.

There are no:
   a. Violations or possible violations of laws or regulations whose effects should be considered for disclosure in the financial statements or as a basis for recording a loss contingency.
   b. Unasserted claims or assessments that our lawyer has advised us are probable of assertion and must be disclosed in accordance with FASB Statement No. 5, Accounting for Contingencies.

Continued

Peach Blossom Cologne Company
Letter of Representations
December 31, 2008

L.O.R./E-6
3 of 4
2-5-09
JWP

Page Three

    c. Other liabilities or gain or loss contingencies that are required to be accrued or disclosed by FASB Statement No. 5.

The Company had no other contingent or possible liabilities that have not been disclosed to you.

Purchase and Sales Commitments:
At December 31, 2008, the Company had no important unfilled contracts for purchases in excess of normal requirements or at prices substantially in excess of market, or for sales at prices that are expected to result in a loss.

Capital Stock:
All capital stock issued or reserved for options, warrants, or other future issuance is disclosed in the financial statements.

Minutes:
We have made available to you (1) all financial records and related data, and (2) minutes of the meetings of stockholders, directors, and committees of directors, or summaries of actions of recent meetings for which minutes have not yet been prepared. Minutes of such meetings as exhibited to you are complete and authentic records of all such meetings held during the period from January 1, 2008 through December 31, 2008.

General:
No events have occurred and no facts have been discovered since December 31, 2008, which would make the balance sheet at that date or the statement of earnings for the year then ended materially inaccurate or misleading.

No charges are pending against the Company for alleged violations of federal, state, or local laws, which would have any material effect on the financial statements. No communications from regulatory agencies have been received concerning noncompliance with or deficiencies in financial reporting practices.

The company has complied with all aspects of contractual agreements that would have a material effect on the financial statements in the event of noncompliance.

No director, officer, or principal holder of the Company's equity securities was indebted (except for minor amounts for ordinary travel and expenses) to the Company at any time during the year.

The following have been properly recorded or disclosed in the financial statements:
    a. Related-party transactions, including sales, purchases, loans, transfers, leasing arrangements,

Continued

Peach Blossom Cologne Company
Letter of Representations
December 31, 2008

L.O.R./E-6
4 of 4
2-5-09
JWP

Page Four

   and guarantees, and amounts receivable from or payable to related parties.
b. Guarantees, whether written or oral, under which the company is contingently liable.
c. Significant estimates and material concentrations known to management that are required to be disclosed in accordance with the AICPA's Statement of Position 94-6 (Disclosure of Certain Significant Risks and Uncertainties). (Significant estimates are estimates at the balance sheet date that could change materially within the next year; concentrations refer to volumes of business, revenues, available sources of supply, or markets or geographic areas for which events could occur that would significantly disrupt normal finances within the next year.)

Internal Control:

We confirm that we are responsible for establishing and maintaining adequate internal control over financial reporting. We have prepared a separate report on internal control over financial reporting in compliance with section 404 of the Sarbanes-Oxley Act of 2002.

Very truly yours,

   Lawrence Lancaster
   President
Peach Blossom Cologne Company

   Parker Shelton
   Controller
Peach Blossom Cologne Company

Inquiry was made of Mr. Lancaster, President, Mr. Shelton, Controller, and Ms. Stockton, Treasurer, concerning possible contingent liabilities and events occurring subsequent to the balance sheet date that may require accrual or disclosure in the financial statement.

The client's legal counsel, Edwards, Overstreet, and Gilley reported in their letter to us (Schedule (A.L./E-5)) that they knew of no direct or contingent liabilities arising from past or present litigation.

I also examined the minutes of the meetings of the Board of Directors and the client's contract files, inquired of management, and reviewed subsequent year's journals and ledgers, searching for possible contingent liabilities and subsequent events. Nothing was found to indicate the existence of any contingent liabilities or subsequent events.

On the basis of my examination, it is my opinion that no contingent liabilities exist at 12-31-08 and that no subsequent events have occurred requiring accrual or disclosure.

Jasper W. Parsons
Audit Senior
February, 5, 2009

I reviewed all cash vouchers and supporting documents for the period 1-1-09 to 1-9-09, as well as unmatched invoice and receiver files for the period 1-1-09 to 1-23-09. No January vouchers represented merchandise or services prior to January 1, 2009, except as noted on W/P (E-2).

A review of transactions within the interest and professional fees operating accounts, as well as a review of the minutes of the Board of Directors' meetings, indicated that there were no unrecorded note obligations or litigation contingencies.

Confirmation from client's legal counsel indicated that no pending litigation, direct, or contingent liabilities exist for the Company. Reference attorney's letter (A.L./E-5).

A letter of representations was obtained. Regarding liabilities, that letter indicated that all direct liabilities of the company were recorded and all contingent liabilities had been disclosed to our auditing firm. The letter revealed no apparent unrecorded liabilities. The letter of representations is referenced (L.O.R./E-6).

Standard bank confirmations were obtained. The Big City National Bank confirmation identified a note payable to that bank. This note was recorded by the client as indicated on W/P (F-1).

Excerpts from minutes of the Board of Directors' meetings are included in the permanent file materials. The minutes revealed no items resulting in unrecorded liabilities.

Accordingly, no unrecorded liabilities were found.

Jasper W. Parsons
Audit Senior
February 5, 2009